Law, Culture&
Africana Studies

Africana Studies:
A Review of Social Science Research

Editor

James L. Conyers, Jr., University of Houston

Assistant Editor

Dr. Andrew Smallwood, Austin Peay University

Graduate Assistants

Kady Kante, Leah McAlister Shields, University of Houston

Book Review Editor

Dr. Christel Temple, Maryland at Baltimore County,
an Honors College

Law, Culture& Africana Studies

Edited by
James L. Conyers, Jr.

Africana Studies,
Volume 2

Transaction Publishers
New Brunswick (U.S.A.) and London (U.K.)

Library of Congress Catalog Number: 2007017373
ISBN: 978-1-14128-0660-2
Printed in the United States of America

Library of Congress Cataloging-in-Publication Data

Law, culture, and Africana studies / edited by James L. Conyers, Jr.
    p. cm.
  Includes index.
  ISBN 978-1-4128-0660-2
  1. African Americans—Study and teaching (Higher) 2. African Americans—Social conditions. 3. African Americans—Civil rights. 4. African Americans—Intellectual life. 5. African American arts. 6. Africa—Study and teaching (Higher) I. Conyers, James L.

E184.7.L39 2007
305.896'073—dc22   2007017373

Contents

1

Elijah Muhammad's Nation of Islam: Separatism, Regendering, and a Secular Approach to Black Power after Malcolm X (1965-1975)

Ula Y. Taylor

Why would anyone become a member of the Nation of Islam after the assassination of Malcolm X (El-Hajj Malik El-Shabazz) on February 21, 1965, in New York's Audubon Ballroom? More than any other leader, Malcolm X stood at the ideological vortex in the dynamic movement for black liberation. His fiercely smart rhetoric helped to shift the dominant political struggle from a strategy of civil rights liberalism to eclectic expressions of Black Nationalism. As the most charismatic and visible spokesperson for the Nation of Islam, Malcolm moved beyond the Honorable Elijah Muhammad's (the Nation of Islam's undisputed leader from 1934 to 1975) call for economic self-sufficiency nationalism. Combining an application of armed self-defense "by any means necessary" (in a political climate that hosed racist government repression in the form of the state police) along with a lethal critique of white folks as "devils," Malcolm appealed to the most socially isolated, politically dispossessed, and economically desperate members of the black proletariat. It was Malcolm's undivided commitment to create a powerful group of "believers" in the Nation of Islam that resulted in a substantial membership increase. In 1955, there were only sixteen temples largely located in the urban North, but by 1960 over fifty temples were sprinkled throughout the United States with registered membership estimated between 50,000 and 250,000.[1]

Malcolm has become a militant martyr for the Nation of Islam and a "Black Power paradigm—the archetype, reference point, and spiritual

1

adviser in absentia for a generation of Afro-American activist."[2] This chapter explores a number of issues, including the Nation of Islam's views of Africa, reparations, land as well as poverty and progress. Its focus is on these issues of separatism and the redefinition of gender roles—the creation of two allegedly complementary subjects, a masculine man and a feminine woman.[3] Clearly, Black Power advocates had multiple visions, but the Nation of Islam provides one of the most imaginative sites to explore their concerns about intimate gender relations, or what Paulette Pierce insight fully calls "boudoir politics," and the creation of a "black nation." This article is an effort to complicate our understanding of African-American identity, political subjectivity, gender prescriptions, and nation building during the peak of the modern Black Power movement. Furthermore, I suggest that in the post-Malcolm X period, the religious nature of the Nation of Islam was not the major impetus for new membership. Above all, the Nation of Islam's secular programs, promising power and wealth, were the key to its expansion.

A Nation within a Nation

It is through a consideration of historical shifts in the Nation of Islam that one can locate key transformations and continuities in the meaning of Black Power. The formative years of the Nation of Islam (1930s) developed within a milieu of restrictive, second-class citizenship for African-Americans. W.D. Fard Muhammad, the founder and self-proclaimed prophet of the Nation of Islam, was known by his followers as a divine black messiah (Allah in the flesh), and he designated Elijah Muhammad as his last "Messenger."[4] An unorthodox version of Islam, the Nation of Islam is usually studied outside the general scope of Muslim life despite the efforts of followers to draw on orthodox Islam and Islamic cultural representations such as symbolism, extensive numerology, and codes of appropriate living. Similar to devout Muslims, Nation of Islam members conducted all daily activities with reference to religion. Although their faith was not anchored in the recitation of Arabic prayers, Islam became an organizing force that produced a community of "believers" determined to resist the bulwarks of Jim Crow (economic repression, political disenfranchisement, and social ostracism) by building an empowered independent nation within the United States. Black people, Fard Muhammad explained, were the "original" people on the planet who ruled from "Asia." Historian Claude Clegg underscores that Fard Muhammad believed "the use of the word Africa to denote what he called East Asia" was a ploy by "whites to divide people of color who were, in his view, all Asiatic."[5] The "so-called American Negro" was in fact an "Asiatic Blackman, the maker, the owner, the cream of the planet earth, God or the universe." [6] Fard Muhammad invented a history that disconnected black people in the United States from Africa and Africans, thereby detaching them from the Western imagination of blackness, which was loaded with demeaning stereotypes of African "savagery" and dehumanizing slavery.[7] At the same time, this narrative failed to critique colonialist descriptions of black Africans as "uncivilized"; rather, Fard Muhammad's rhetoric often accentuated negative myths. In effect, early Nation of Islam members wanted to build a modern black nation from a glorification of "Asiatic blackness" and a rejection of sub-Saharan Africa. This ideological structure expresses not only the internalization of black Africa as "backward," but also the very real alienation that Nation of Islam members felt as a result of colonialism, slavery, and Jim Crow. Thus, as Robert Reid Pharr avers, the Nation of Islam's history produced an identity for black Americans that was "imagined as larger than blackness," even though "very few others are allowed to share this identity.[8]

The elevation of black Americans most notably above black Africans paralleled the collective gouging of Caucasians as "white, blue-eyed devils" who were "grafted out of Black people specifically to bedevil the planet."[9] Fard Muhammad advocated a separate nation from Caucasians, a place where its members were protected from a Jim Crow government and all of the "sins" from the "devil." After he mysteriously disappeared in 1934 from Detroit (the Nation of Islam's center), Elijah Muhammad continued this millennialistic mission to reject the devil's institutions. A complete withdrawal from American society was presumed to be the key to the resurrection of black people. So, when President Franklin D. Roosevelt instituted social security in the late 1930s, "the Messenger" told his members to refuse the identification numbers since they were the mark of the beast. For Muhammad, social security digits not only kept individuals under surveillance but were also no different from the surnames black folks had inherited from slavery. Both systems of identification represented white domination. The federal government became redefined white domination.

Given that there was no area of policies, economic, and social life where legal segregation did not intrude, scholar Ernest Allen concludes that converts to the Nation of Islam viewed "federal and state agencies as uninstalled repositories of satanic influence."[10] The rejection of such institutions was a critique of both white supremacy and modernity. Nation of Islam leaders had responded to colonial notions the black people were outside of Western modernity, with a general repugnance toward their modern structures. Moreover, Elijah Muhammad's incessant emphasis on a particular brand of Islam, a religion that allegedly accorded black people respect and worth because men were successful patriarchal heads of their homes and women were the epitome of feminine modesty, distinguished and ultimately severed his subjects from an ostensibly corrupt nation of hypocritical white Christians.[11] Nation of Islam followers clearly defined their enemy in both racial and religious terms.

After Malcolm's 1952 prison parole, his talent was used specifically to start new temples in Boston and Philadelphia, as well as bolster membership in sagging ones. Within two years, Elijah Muhammad rewarded Malcolm's efforts by assigning him the most coveted temple outside of Chicago, Temple No. 7 in Harlem. It was in New York City that Malcolm's influence reached new heights. As the Nation of Islam's most public Minister, Malcolm proselytized not only among the hustlers, pimps, prostitutes, drug dealers, and thieves but also in churches and at political debates. He contended that the teaching of the Honorable Elijah Muhammad explained that black folks were impoverished and ethically lacking because white racists conscientiously withheld their access to "self" and neglected their most fundamental needs. After vividly detailing the failures of white America, Malcolm provided the foundation for the so called Negroes to understand that they were indeed the chosen, the supreme of humankind, and that the key to their resurrection could be found in the Nation of Islam. He used his own wayward life history as a powerful example. Malcolm had sold drugs, stolen, and ended up in jail, but after he converted to the Nation of Islam while in prison (1946-52), his whole attitude and outlook on life changed. Listening to his emotionally stirring and candid testimony, Malcolm's devotes were able to recognize aspects of themselves, which pulled them closer to him and his Black Nationalist revelation. John Edgar Wireman argues that Malcolm delivered a message during the sixties that was "as absolute as the message runaway slaves delivered to Ole Massa." Malcolm, however, "wasn't running and his direction was not away but toward a future, a center we're still struggling to glimpse."[12]

Prior to his brutal death (Black Muslims who had been implicated in the killing were quickly dismissed by the Nation of Islam leadership as FBI infiltrators and hypocrites), Malcolm wrote in his 1964 autobiography that he knew, "[as] any official in the Nation of Islam would instantly have known, any death talk could have been approved of if not actually initiated by only one man," the Honorable Elijah Muhammad. No doubt, Malcolm was a loyal convert, and prior to being ousted (in November 1963, after the assassination of President John F. Kennedy) from the Nation of Islam, his deepest personal belief, was that Elijah Muhammad in every aspect of his being was a symbol of moral, mental, and spiritual reform among the American black people.[13] In hindsight, Malcolm told photographer Gordon Parks that as a messenger's national minister and most visible spokesperson, he had done many things to his regret because he was a zombie and like all Muslims he was hypnotized pointed in a certain direction and told to march.[14] By 1964, Malcolm and others had critiqued Elijah Muhammad as an adulterer who betrayed his followers, the Nation of Islam as an organization that was moving too slow, and Islam as too inactive.[15] It is difficult to fathom that during this very volatile public moment and thereafter a steady stream of women and men continued to be drawn into the Nation of Islam's fold.[16] Refugees from a variety of political groups who sought a structured black political organization swelled the ranks of the Nation of Islam, as the call for Black Power resonated throughout the United States. By 1965, the Nation of Islam continued to represent a religious answer to problems of poverty and racial discrimination, but also a conservative capitalist solution to these difficult circumstances. Under Elijah Muhammad's leadership the Nation of Islam principles and demands had crystallized. "If you want money, good homes, and friendships in all walks of life, come and follow me," said the messenger.[17] His bountiful membership call yielded a favorable response among black folks who had northern Promised Land. They lived in dilapidated housing projects infested with drugs and hopelessness, representing generations of economically depressed people. More to the point, the Nation of Islam's platform offered a life chord for black people who were untouched by civil rights victories. The messenger cultivated an atmosphere of support and caring for his followers, and numerous testimonies by members suggest that he made good on his promise to improve the conditions of those who believe. The Nation of Islam converts explain that their lives were plagued by drugs, alcohol, and lack of discipline and morals but the messenger had extended kindness to them when others only condemned their behavior. Inside the prisons, Elijah Muhammad would make sure that jailed converts received encouraging letters, and Malcolm X recalled how he sent money all over the country to prison inmates who write to him.[18] Brother Thomas 18X of Chicago explained that, "For many years, the Messenger has provided us with jobs" and he "has taught us how to have peace of mind, friendship, money and decent homes."[19] Under the guidance of the messenger, members remark that they had become "successful" in terms of employment and had progressed in terms of knowing "self." Sister Joan X remembered that the first time that she visited the Nation of Islam's Chicago headquarters in 1972, "it was indeed heaven on earth, all of your needs were met by sophisticated people who looked like you."[20]

Black Power

Even though activists had battled to give substance to the newly acquired social (Civil Rights Act of 1964) and political (Voting Rights Act of 1965) rights of citizenship, many of the younger freedom fighters attended college and were experiencing an increasing sense of disillusionment within the movement. Only a small percentage of middle-class black people had reaped the benefits of legal change while the predicament of the masses seemed to worsen. Occupying a precarious class position, most college students were financially strapped, but a middle-class status was within their grasp via their degrees. As a blossoming middle stratum, student activists struggled to transform institutions that produced inequalities, but at the same time they recognized that their higher degrees would position them to seize certain elite advantages. Constructing an identity within a cauldron of inequalities is difficult. Sister Joan 4X spoke for many when she said, "Many of us wonder what we'll do without education when we leave college." [21] They were not alone in terms of feeling ambiguous about their future. The urban rebellions that spread throughout the country, beginning with the Watts uprising front days after the passage of the August 1965 Voting Rights Act, evidenced the demoralization and alienation Northern black people felt in America as a result of poverty and Gestapo style policing.

The Student Nonviolence Coordinating Committee (SNCC) members certainly understood the frustrations of black urbanites. Beginning in 1960, they had courageously put their bodies on the line at sit in demonstrations and on freedom ride treks, but by 1965 many of them were pessimistic and felt influential black leaders were willing to settle for tokens of racial progress. After electing Stokely Carmichael chairman in 1966, SNCC workers, especially the newly formed Atlanta Project staff, began to insist that black people think in terms of Black Power in order to squash white power. An observer recalled that SNCC members in good standing during this period had digested Frantz Fanon's *The Wretched of the Earth*, which described the "Western man decadent and therefore not to be emulated by colonized peoples" and they could quote at length from Malcolm X Speaks.[22] In the tense aftermath of Malcolm's death in 1965, other political organizations also began to reshape, in the case of the Congress of Racial Equality (CORE), and new organizations were created, notably the Black Panther Party, the Republic of New Africa, Revolutionary Action Movement, and the League of Revolutionary Black Workers. Black Nationalist and separatist ideas, as well as armed self defense, were designed to give real meaning to Malcolm's legacy and Black power. The postmortem period erupted between these groups regarding the most effective way to destroy white hegemony, the Nation of Islam hunkered down and simply pushed to further implement its insular nationhood goals. With a long history of racial self determination, cultural autonomy, and black capitalism, the Nation of Islam was able to quickly rebound from the taint of Malcolm's deaths to an organization that was seen by many activists as the separatist vanguard. Given that activists were looking for basic, but fundamentally key, elements of Black Power, it is not surprising that they spent the post 1965 period searching for an organization that at its core celebrated a black identity and empowered black people on their own terms.

Anna Karriem's political activism illustrates how the problematic dynamics within the Black Power movement could initiate a conversion to the Nation of Islam. She had been a devoted member of SNCC between 1964 and 1967 and worked to bring political power to black people in Alabama and Mississippi counties. On Election Day in 1967, however, she witnessed how local registrars held loaded guns to drive SNCC members off, and black sharecroppers were driven off of their land and forbidden to take anything with them because they had voted for a black candidate. Karriem found herself, along with other SNCC workers and members of the homeless families, driving stakes into the ground and building a wooden floor, so that we could set up tents to get them out of the cold. After 1966, under the leadership of Carmichael, SNCC efforts were to obtain political and economic freedom for black people, and Karriem states that they were willing to arm themselves for revolution in the streets. Teaching that "freedom comes from the barrel of a gun," SNCC leadership, Karriem argued, did not teach the outcome of armed revolution by Black people nor did it teach Black people in Los Angeles in 1965 how to restore their burned homes and businesses in Watts. Karriem was also critical of Carmichael for not coming around to teach the people in Detroit and Newark in 1967 who revolted against slum living and unemployment how to do for themselves in the way of rebuilding their burned communities. Black power too often led to black deaths, she concluded. Karriem accepted Islam as taught by Elijah Muhammad, because she was tired of the destruction caused by so called Black leaders who expound on ideas that had no foundation in reality. The messenger taught converts that ideology is the science of ideas we have had four hundred years to come up with ideas.[23] Karriem summarized that the Nation of Islam had mobbed beyond ideological rhetoric and call for revolution; their efforts had yielded small businesses, schools, and farmland and no one had been displayed in the process. Sister Karriem also convinced other women activists to pledge loyalty to the Nation of Islam. Sister Marguerite X met Karriem while a student activist at Tuskegee. Before attending the mosque, Marguerite X was of the "radical group of college students."[24] Marguerite and Karriem's conversion helps us to understand how the Nation of Islam's conservative vision of action took on revolutionary meaning within a context of effete political resistance and racist violence.

Brother Preston (X) Dixon's experience also sheds additional light on an activist's conversion to the Nation of Islam. He had become involved with the Black Student Union (BSU) in Los Angeles, and the first inkling that something was amiss came when the BSU central committee established a constitution and philosophy that was based on the program of the Most Honorable Elijah Muhammad—Wants and Beliefs.[25] The Black Panther Party for Self Defense, organized in Oakland, California, October 1966, had also replicated the Nation of Islam's "Wants and Beliefs" platform in its "Ten-Point Program."[26] Huey Newton had attended mosques in both San Francisco and Oakland, spoke fairly often to a number of members, and regularly read the Nation of Islam's popular weekly newspaper, *Muhammad Speaks*. Newton would have joined then, but he could not deal with their religion. He had been raised in a fairly strict Christian home and had had enough of religion and could not bring himself to adopt another one. [27] Dixon was not turned off by the religious aspect of the nation of Islam, but he admits that the "changeover was not immediate," for there was still considerable doubt within him. The point of no return came later when his local BSU organized a program and only brothers from the Nation of Islam would travel and speak to his group for free. Well known BSU leadership, to Dixon's disgust, usually required local chapters to pay for airfare, lodging, plus honorarium. Spreading the message of Black Power soon became a fundraising tactic for some of its leadership. After 1966, Carmichael took to the speaking circuit and in most un-Snick like fashion, insisted on traveling first class on airplanes and receiving a thousand dollar honorarium for a lecture. His popularity and his appearance as a gadfly in public debates about civil rights soon earned him the nickname by friends and foes of Steely "Star Michael."[28] Brother Minister Billy X, on the other hand, was willing to travel some 200 miles, and his requirements were just a chance to speak and teach Islam. In turn, Dixon began attending the local Nation of Islam mosque and reading Muslim literature, "almost for the start I found myself searching for answers, and simultaneously, becoming aware of how foolish I had acted and sounded when I demanded the same person who had robbed me of the knowledge of myself, teach me back into the knowledge of myself."[29] Disgusted with displays of selfishness and ignorance, Dixon served his relation with the "BSU and stood up under the banner of Islam."[30] Following the 1965 "summer of discontent," other new converts recall how their Nation of Islam membership was directly linked to disappointment in other political organizations, but particularly the newly formed BSU that had spread like wildfire and, therefore, were the least structurally organized. Sister Lindsay Bryant remembered how she was initially involved in the BSU at the University of California, Santa Barbara, because she sought an organization that would give her identity as a black woman. Working diligently to obtain a better education system and a better world in which to live, Bryant soon understood that the slogan by any means necessary to achieve the BSU goals ironically translated into "sleeping with whites and allowing them to integrate into our ranks."[31] Bryant began attending the local mosque and became more insipid every time she went. Completely disillusioned with the BSU and the "phenomenal of resolution," Bryant also became convinced that the BSU did not have the solution to the Blacks problems so she decided to unite behind one leader and the only man qualified to lead the so called American Negro was the "Honorable Elijah Muhammad."[32]

Sister Joan 4X also came to the Nation of Islam after membership in the BSU because she was constantly in search of the "qualities embodied in the Nation." Growing up in the South made her aware of the evils and atrocities that white men do to people every day of our waking lives. Joan 4X readily admits that she was not quite ready for the Caucasians on the west coast for they have placed a "mental fog over the minds of our people that is much worse than any physical danger." This crisis pushed Joan 4X to become a poor example to the new breed of black student trying desperately to rid themselves of the devil's influence. Putting her on the line and housing that she was Black and proud to white administrators and officials meant that she also had to have the courage to do something truly unique about the condition in the United States. As an intelligent person, she analyzed how efficiently the white man uses the media to choose our leaders and they brainwash them and students. After becoming a member of the Nation of Islam, Joan 4X argued that the white press served as a decoy to keep black folks from the only true leader in America, the messenger. For Joan 4X, *The Autobiography of Malcolm X* (1964) was the most "obvious sign" to her that the devil knows, "Islam is the only salvation for black people and the only vehicle that really unites us." Pointing out that when Malcolm X taught Islam, "devils couldn't do enough to blaspheme him and the whole program of the Messenger; but when the man turned from the light of Islam, and especially now that he is dead, the white press can't put enough copies of his autobiography in the hands of our peoples."[33]

It is somewhat ironic that the Nation of Islam's platform was interpreted as a Black Power blueprint and that the waves of new members were former student activists, considering the fact that Elijah Muhammad never wavered from his conservative position that his followers eschew mainstream politics. Searching for answers to complicated, multilayered questions produced a longing to belong to something meaningful. Black Power activists were able to fill this lacuna by pushing the idea that black people at home and throughout the diaspora shared a collective identity and origins rooted in Africa. But Elijah Muhammad taught that Africans were a backward and uncivilized people and that the so-called negro in the United States was in fact the most civilized and superior member of the human race. The diatribe against Africa at times sounded like racist, colonial gibberish but removers who may have disagreed with him were afraid to speak out against their leader. One Pan African leader, Queen Mother Moore of Harlem, recalled how Malcolm X told her that before he could say the word Africa it would have to come from Elijah.[34] This was a highly unlikely possibility since, as Malcolm X put it, Elijah Muhammad "was as anti African as he was anti white." In fact, Malcolm X adds, "he never had one statement that was pro-African."[35] Moore concluded that when she spent three days at the home of Elijah Muhammad, they argued because "he didn't want to hear nothing about Africa."[36] The Nation of Islam's assessment of Africa is confusing since historically and during the modern Black power movement, Africa was always imagined as home. The messenger justified his position with the following analysis:

> Many of my people, the so-called Negroes, say we should help the nations of African which are wakening. This has been said as if we owned America. We are so foolish! What part of America do you have that you can offer toward helping Africa? Who is independent, the nations of Africa or we? The best act would be to request the

independent governments of Africa and Asia to help us. We are the ones who need help. We have little or nothing to offer as help to others. We should begin to help at home first.[37]

Locating a home would provide the wellspring of unity, strength, and cultural meaning in the midst of the revolutionary chaos. Converts believed that the Nation of Islam, at the very least, offered a path of solving both personal and societal problems in that it linked Black Nationalist thought with politically transformative action. Black businesses, Muslims, schools, temples, and families were very real, tangible examples of successful nation building. At the same time, followers were encouraged to assertively critique the United States using activist language. For example, Sister Christie Deloris X of Birmingham, Alabama, explained that the white man's civilization can offer us nothing in the way of security, education, and spirituality. In other words, these capitalist fascist racist men colonized society as a whole is fallen as our Beloved Leader and Teacher has taught for more than 40 years."[38] Writer James Baldwin was never a member of the Nation of Islam, yet he was also drawn to Elijah Muhammad's peculiar authority. Slender and small in stature, Muhammad had a smile, Baldwin remembered, that "promised to take the burden of my life off my shoulders."[39]

Separate Territory and Institutions

Black Power advocates who shouted the slogan the loudest, Alvin F. Poussaint argues, "were those with the oldest battle scars from the terror, demoralization and castration which they experienced through continual direct confrontation" with white racism. In addition, these activists also recognized that "racial pride and self love alone do not fill the bellies of starving black children in Mississippi."[40] Convinced that white people would never properly share resources nor conceded full equality, manta in attendance at the 1967 Black power Conference in Newark, New Jersey, called for partitioning of the United States into two separate territories when activists were struggling to dismantle Jim Crow during the 1950s. Understanding that borders would move the Nation of Islam beyond an imagined state, to shame the government into a concession, Muhammad insists that former slave masters were obligated to maintain and supply their needs in a separate territory for the next twenty to twenty-five years, given that their ancestors had earned it. Long before reparations became a popular plank among Black Nationalists, Muhammad and his ministers had demanded compensation for the damaged done to generation of black people as back payment for enslaved labor. Much later, a Black Manifesto was issued at the April 1969 national Black Economic Development Conference in Detroit under the leadership of James Forman, which called upon the White Christian churches and the Jewish synagogues in the United States and all other racist institutions "to give $500 million in reparations and to surrender 60 percent of their assets to the conference to be used for the economic, social, and cultural rehabilitation of the black community."[41]

By 1965, the Nation of Islam had moved beyond cessation rhetoric, buying farmland in three states as well as an abundance of property and small businesses near each of its temples (grocery stores, restaurants, and dry cleaning shops), valued in the millions.[42] The pursuit of economic power through the creation of separate communal institutions was a replication of Galvanism, but in terms of the modern liberation movement, that strategy prefigured the late 1960s black capitalist's goals.[43] Already acting like people with power and control over their won destiny, the institutor built by the Nation of Islam was clear evidence of its material achievements. *Muhammad Speaks* published countless accounts of people who were in the grave of ignorance and poverty before their conversions and how they had made real progress with the Nation of Islam. For example, Brother Charles JX of Detroit says he became inspired to do something for himself after reading Muhammad's *Message to the Blackman* (1965). "Finally the solutions to all of my problems," Brothers Charles recalled, "which had heretofore escape me, became crystal clear." He decided to start a construction business, and he trained his son to become proficient in the field. Until he heard the teaching of Muhammad, he never thought he could have a successful and profitable business in his lifetime.[44] Much of the follower's individual success was connected to the messenger's "Economic Freedom" plan that he introduced in 1964. Members were taught how to economize and save. Followers were told to just save five cents a day or twenty-five cents a week amongst themselves and this would mean millions of dollars per year. At the annual Saviors Day Convention, Muhammad would spell out the distance in dollars and cents that had been accumulated as well as future financial expectations. The relationship between economic success and acquiring a sense of independence and power also had the objective of transforming the mindset of members.

One of the main handicaps identified by the messenger that prevented so-called negroes from achieving success was the lack of knowledge of self. Members have given countless testimonies on how they had been formerly brainwashed; however, the teaching of the Honorable Elijah Muhammad explained their history. Sister Beverly Maurad, National Director of Education for the Nation of Islam in 1971, in a speech to the graduates of Muhammad Universities of Islam (secondary schools) states that even though students study some of the same subjects and read from the same books as their peers, their education is "better-more comprehensive" because "once you have been awakened it is easy to understand." The messenger taught that black people are "the original man, the maker, and the owner of the planet earth. This one fact gives the true student, the true believer, a desire to retain his lost heritage" and "once again become members of a great civilization and Nation." Knowledge of self allows one to "see that you (Blackman) are the ones alluded to in your History Text books as having created wonderful civilizations with marvelous structures and using technological skills." As Black Muslim students, Maurad concludes, they have the advantage because they "know who they are," and thus they are "able to perceive and weigh and balance more clearly the curriculum presented."[45] Not that the Nation of Islam create schools and curriculum "to educate self."

Black Power advocates, many of whom were enrolled or had recently attended college, also insisted on an academic curriculum that reflected the history and culture of black people. The Nation of Islam was already light-years ahead of the activists on this front. For years they had taught the members' children in separate schools that were usually located near the temples. The schools, in many ways, were the glue that held the Nation of Islam together. Sonsyrea Tate discusses how her mother stayed in the Nation of Islam so that she and her siblings would be eligible for the schools.[46] Some college students were drawn to the Nation of Islam largely because of its curriculum. Sister Joan 4X argued that black student demands for black studies departments would never be recognized and the messenger already boldly taught people "Black history."[47] The Nation of Islam's schools also became an important alternative for parents who did not want to have their children vaccinated a requirement for public education. And, after the Tuskegee Study became public knowledge in American men between 1932 to 1972, authorized by the Centers for Disease Control, more African-Americans feared the entire vaccination process; thus, the Nation of Islam schools were an important option.

Clearly, the religious "Islamic" nature of the Nation of Islam was not the major impetus for membership in the post-1965 period. Instead, the Nation of Islam's secular programs and exclusive black membership reinforced the new member's agenda to build a separate black nation. Essentially, Muhammad promised to provide material symbols of power and wealth for people who had been discarded from the American populace and disinherited from the "American dream." By offering black Americans a vanguard lifestyle, Muhammad not only trumped the political struggle to extend rights of citizenship, but as T. H. Marshall would argue, his call was couched in an ideal expression of the modern citizenship, "against which achievements can be measured and toward which aspirations can be directed."[48] Thus, nationhood success was predicated upon establishing a separate existence and presenting Islam as a materially empowering religion; one simply had to become a "Black Muslim" to receive the benefits.

Regendering

The making of the Black Muslim subject involved a complicated set of social relationships and obligations to the Nation of Islam. Whereas there are always rules for belonging, Roger Smith's concept of "civil myths" explains how guidelines of eligibility and exclusion are used to create political communities and thereby reflect their contested inner workings. In the case of the Nation of Islam, membership was rooted in gendered prescriptions. That is, men's and women's roles had to be reconfigured based on gendered stereotypes and hierarchies, and regulated differently in order to achieve black redemption, political emancipation, economic self-sufficiency, and social isolation from whites.

Nationalist precepts of gender promoted a conservative agenda where patriarchy took center stage. A separatist, masculine nation—the representation of a responsible, disciplined, dignified, and defiant manhood—would give black men rights and privileges denied them in white America. The centering of black men, however, pushed black women to the margin of nation building, Placing black women on the periphery served to counter/resist the master narrative of slavery that stereotypically portrays black women as jezebels, matriarchs, and mannish, women's roles that were used to both shame and usurp black manhood. Essentially, for the Nation of Islam, the emasculation of black men and their lack of masculine agency were dialectically connected to hyper sexualized, out-of-control, defiled, black women. According to Elijah Muhammad, "There is no nation on earth that has less respect for and as little control of their women as we so called Negroes here in America."[49]

The building of a Nation required public displays of symbols that often occurred at the site of the body. Representations of difference (men and women were essentially different by "nature") were accompanied by a prescription of particular relationships between men and women. North American slavery had created two types of victims: women who were raped and not allowed a feminine presence under the burdens of capitalism and men who were emasculated and rendered powerless. The reentering of Nation of Islam subjects returned them to a particular sense of "self" that was "natural" and denied under slavery. While a real Nation of Islam man was a masculine breadwinner and a good Nation of Islam woman was a feminine housewife, traditional roles, it was also believed, would bring a form of emotional intimacy between men and women. Boudoir politics recognizes the human need for love, and "any movement that hopes to empower" women and men "as opposed to just mobilize them" must deal with the issue.[50]

The unreal "matriarchal" legacy of slavery endured during the post-1965 Black Power movement largely because of distorted images of black female identity, for instance, the fable that black women were already liberated. Barbara Smith critiques the myth that black women were emancipated in advance of black men because the women shouldered the responsibilities of heading families and working outside the home. Above all, "An ability to cope under the worst conditions is not liberation. Underlying this myth is the assumption that black women are towers of strength who neither fell nor need what other human beings do, either emotionally or materially." This widespread myth, codified in the 1965 Secretary of Labor Daniel Patrick Moynihan Report, insisted that black women had damned themselves and rendered black men "impotent."[51] Black male nationalists, within and outside of the Nation of Islam, presumed that women had to be controlled and assume a passive role in order for men to rise up and be "real men" in the United States. Maulana Ron Karenga led the cultural nationalists with perceptions such as "what make women appealing is femininity and she can't be feminine without being submissive."[52] Moreover, as Akiba ya Elimu states, "The man" should be "the leader of the house/nation because his knowledge of the world is broader, his awareness is greater, his understanding is fuller and his application of this information is wiser," which certainly justifies why he should lead.[53] Nation of Islam male leaders added white women into this garbled misrepresentation. In fact, they accused black women of mimicking the immoral habits of white women. Utilizing racial pride rhetoric as a form of control, the messenger told black men to "stop our women from trying to look like them [white women]. By bleaching, powdering, ironing and coloring their hair, painting their lips, cheeks, and eyebrows; wearing shorts; going half-nude in public places. Stop women from using unclean language in public (and at home), from smoking and drug addiction habits."[54] In sum, slavery as well as the behavior of aggressive Western women had brought destruction to Allah's social order, generating renegade black women.

Restraining women, also an obsession among Middle Eastern Islamic fundamentalist, positions the Nation of Islam squarely in line with the patriarchal climate of Black Power. Muhammad, however, helped to camouflage the gender inequalities in the Nation of Islam with the affectionate rhetoric of love, protection, and respect for black womanhood. This is an important point, especially considering the scathing, sexual criticism of black women at the time. One simply has to recall Stokely Carmichael's response to a question concerning the "proper position of women in SNCC." He jokingly replied, "prone." Or, more to the point, the views uttered by Eldridge Cleaver, leader of the BPP, are without a doubt the most misogynistic. He wrote that he knew that "the white man made the black woman the symbol of slavery." In his mind, this view explained his lack of attraction and respect for black women. He gloated, "The only way that I can bust my nuts with a black bitch is to close my eyes and pretend that she is Jezebel. If I was to look down and see a black bitch underneath me or if my hand happened to feel her nappy hair, that would be the end, it would be all over."[55] Paulette Pierce insightfully analyzes that such were the most influential musings of the fertile imagination of Black Nationalists during the sixties as they labored to "birth a free nation or die in the process."[56]

Within this climate, according to *Muhammad Speaks*, some women viewed the Nation of Islam as a safe, loving "home." Sister Charles Ann X said that "Islam elevates that so-called Negro woman by giving her wisdom, knowledge, culture and refinement."[57] No longer did Sandra JX consider herself "just a simple, southern girl," but in the Nation of Islam she was "the queen of the entire planet earth and the mother of all civilizations."[58] Sister Vera X Lewis testified that the messenger was "not afraid to point out how the black woman has been abused for some 400 years." She was thankful that her leader "instills in black men a rebirth to their natural urge to protect black women." White men "or even misguided black men can no longer use black women for ill purposes," remarked Lewis. Historically, black women's bodies have been commoditized as legal property and their sexuality exploited to justify capitalism and the peers desires of men.

Sister Mable X recalled how her body, now that she was a member of the Nation of Islam "was overtaken with warmth and beauty." She became "very proud, resourceful, and thankful."[59] It seems that it did not matter (or matter enough to prevent membership) to these women that under the conditions of the Nation of Islam (as well as other black nationalist organizations) respect for their personhood and protection from seething forces hinged on their complete obedience to all paternal figures.

There are indeed complicated reasons why Nation of Islam women accepted what appears to be a second-class status. Aaronetta X Anderson remembered that, when she was on the outside looking in before joining in 1966, she had many misconceptions concerning the role of women. As "quite an assertive person, and seeing how aggressive the brothers were, I assumed women had to take a back seat." After attending the Muslim's Girls Training and General Civilization Classes (MGT-GCG), it became apparent to her that it was "not so much a back seat as the proper seat."[60] The fact that the backseat had to be addressed indicated that women had to be convinced that they were not being subjugated, and that most efficient way to rationalize limiting the participation of women was through an ideology that connected their marginalized role to the greater good of black people. It was both their racial and religious duty to sacrifice self for the liberation project. Sister Melva J.X. Walker of Oklahoma City, Oklahoma says it best. Prior to becoming a register Muslim on June 7, 1971, she always wanted to be famous and beautiful. Her goal was to be a "career woman, successful, progressive and productive." Determined to finish college, she wanted to "find her place and really contribute something valuable to this existing system." After receiving her "X" she understood "exactly that to progress is not just climbing to the top to the devil society, but it means helping her people." The most efficient way to help was to know her place and that place is not on some stage displaying herself, or having her name up in lights, and neither is that place any one of the many careers which she considered from "Ambassador to Africa, to a Playboy bunny," but it is a place where she wanted to spend her life, "Being a Woman, a Natural Black Woman in the Nation of Islam."[61]

Women like Sister Melba J. X. Walker must have faced a major struggle as they transferred their allegiance from organizations that thrived on elevating Africa to one that viewed Africa as backward. Most of the post-1965 Nation of Islam converts first attended the mosque, which usually had pews as opposed to prayer rugs, and wore African apparel and Afro hairstyles. Elijah Muhammad did not approve of this thought dismissal.

He concluded that "if men and women are not satisfied with the styles I give them then I am not satisfied with you being my follower."[62] Islam is a very public and visible religion, and Muhammad was clear about his dictator role as regulator of the material culture and demeanor of his followers. There was little room within the Nation of Islam to challenge prescribed practice or act as a critical citizen.

Clothing was marked as a particularly important sign of Nation of Islam identity and a means for the control over bodies and body image. Like colonial images of Africa, many Nation of Islam converts viewed Africans as a population in need of civilization and lacking in respectability. Elijah Muhammad ordered Nation of Islam men and women to be respectable and civilized through the adoption of a strict dress code. Men were extremely mean, and their uniform consisted of dark colored suits, usually adorned with the messenger's signature bow tie. Long hair was seen by the messenger as a woman's style, and he would not tolerate his followers wearing such germ catchers as dreads. "Stop imitating the non modern man," said Muhammad. "Cut off that pillow of hair behind your head, at the nape of your neck and trim your hair line around the back of your neck like modern man."[63] Women were remobilized to wear long gowns and matching head wraps. This uniform was reminiscent of the Black Cross Nurses of the Garvey movement. Although an expression of their link to Black Nationalism, this attire also kept women within the appropriate Muslim style, covering them from wrist to ankle. It was only a matter of time before members who initially wore colorful dashikis came to accept the messenger's stringent dress code as appropriate. Sister Marguerite X testified that she was one of those Afro-wearers and was of the opinion that Africans or so called Negroes imitating Africans was the only beautiful way of life. "I was wrong."[64] Sister Evelyn X states: "If you see a woman dressed as a Muslim sister, you will think that she is a Muslim and treat her with the respect due a Muslim woman. By the same token, if you see a woman dressed in hot pants, halter top, afro puff wigs on her head, and mud packed on her face, you will think that she must be a loose woman and will treat her as one."[65] The tailored clothing not only combated the sexually deviant myths associated with black people but also gave the appearance of a civilized community with outward forms of religiosity.

Islamic law, as taught by Elijah Muhammad, rested upon the most conservative verse in the Qur'an which dictated that wives should be obedient to their husbands. Muslims scholars debate the meaning of obedience and whether it is a requirement of good behavior rather than submission. Scholar Haleh Afshar states that in practice, Muslim women must accept many of the dictates of patriarchy if they are to accept Islam and its teachings."[66] In 1965, Elijah Muhammad admitted that in some cities the conversation ratio was as high as five men to one woman. But he reasoned that low female support may contribute to the destruction of the black woman by the serpent the devil, dragon, Satan," the forces of white manipulation and not the male centered of the Nation of Islam.

Conclusion

The Nation of Islam was so irritating for men because no one articulated the aspirations of the so-called Negros better than Malcolm X. The need to create a new political source of black personhood and solidarity propelled activists to transform the liberation movement after his assassination. Unfortunately, a host of Black Power organizations, fraught with neophyte leadership, nepotism, and crippling masculinity, rapidly surfaced during the postmortem period. Disappointment and contention within the Black Power ranks ironically gave way to an enhanced sense of the Nation of Islam as a radical political alternative. Elijah Muhammad and his ministers weathered the tense aftermath of Malcolm's death by capitalizing on activists' disillusionment. Cultivating a constellation of theory (original "Asiatic Blackman" and "Black woman" as a "queen of the Universe") and practice (small business and schools), Elijah Muhammad was able to shift the focus away from Malcolm's demise and onto tangible evidence of nation building. The Nation of Islam became a complicated expression of Black Power, and it enables us to consider the intricate production and manifestation of political subjectivity, vis-à-vis gender, race, class, and nation. In the end, the Nation of Islam offered young people who were constructing a political identity and searching for a stable political home a structured, separatist organization committed to a distinctive moral and religious sensibility. Civil agitation assumed the form of Malcolm's legato made black folks aware of the Nation of Islam, but it was his teacher's vision that brought activist into its folds during the post-1965 period.

Notes

1. E. U. Essien Udon, *Black Nationalism: A Search for Identity in America* (Chicago: University of Chicago Press, 1962), 3783.
2. Claude Clegg, *An Original Man: The Life and Times of Elijah Muhammad* (New York: St. Martin Press, 1998), 239 William L. Van Debug, *New day in Babylon: The Black power Movement and American Culture, 1965-1975*(Chicago: The University of Chicago Press, 1992), 2.

3.   For the most part, my sources on the reasons why women and men joined the Nation of Islam in the post-Malcolm X period are limited to an analysis of the Nation of Islam's weekly newspaper *Muhammad Speaks*. In terms of why they joined the organization, the member's testimonies are open to a number or interpretations—some of which I have not yet had time to explore.

4.   The Nation of Islam had been founded in 1930 UN Detroit under W.D. Fred. See Erdmann Doane Beynon, "The Voodoo Cult among Negro Migrants in Detroit," *American Journal of Sociology* 63 (1938). For a discussion of the early years and Elijah Muhammad's meteoric rise, see Claude Clegg, *An Original Man.*

5.   Clegg, *An Original Man*, 48.

6.   Ibid., 42.

7.   For example, see Winthrop Jordan, *White over Black: American Attitudes toward the Negro, 1550-1812* (Baltimore, MD: Penguin Books, 1969).

8.   Robert Reid-Pharr, "Speaking through Anti-Semitism: The Nation of Islam and the Poetics of Black (Counter) Modernity" *Social Text* 14:4 (Winter 1996): 140.

9.   Salem Mauwakkil, "The Nation of Islam and Me," in *The Farrakhan Factor: African American Writers on Leadership, Nationhood and Minister Louis Farrakhan.* Amy Alexander, ed. (New York: Grove Press, 1998), 296.

10.   Ernest Allen, "Minister Louis Farrakhan and the Continuing Evolution of the Nation of Islam" in *The Farrakhan Factor*, 78. Amy Alexander, ed. (New York: Grove Press, 1998), 296.

11.   An Important millennial ideal is that a devil stands between God's people and the heavenly kingdom. See Perry E. Giannakos, "The Black Muslims: An American Millennialistic Response to Racism and Cultural Denigrations," *The Centennial Review* 23:4 (fall 1979): 439.

12.   John Edgar Wideman, "Malcolm X: The Art of Autobiography," in *Malcolm X: In Our Image.* Joe Wood, ed. (New York: Grove press, 1964), 113.

13.   Malcolm X, "The Violent End of the Man Called Malcolm X," *Life* 58:9 (March 5, 1965): 29.

14.   Gordon Parks, "The Violent End of the Man Called Malcolm X," *Life* 58:9 (March 5, 1965).

15.   Malcolm X, *The Autobiography of Malcolm X*, 294-295, 316.

16.   It is extremely difficult to document the numbers of people who left the Nation of Islam, as well as new members, during the post-1965 period. What is evident is that the Nation of Islam continued to be a thriving, separatist organization.

17.   Elijah Muhammad, "Mr. Muhammad Calls for Unified Front of Black Men at New York City Rally," *Pittsburg Courier*, July 19, 1958, 6.

18.   Malcolm X, *The Autobiography of Malcolm X*, 169. New York: Grove Press.

19.   Brother Tomas 18X, "United Under Light of Islam," *Muhammad Speaks* December 29, 1967, 25.

20.   Interview by Ula Taylor of Joan X, October 21, 1999, Oakland, Calif.

21.   Joan 4X, "What Islam Has Done for Me," *Muhammad Speaks*, August 29, 1969, 17.

22.   Gene Roberts, "The Story of Snick: From Freedom High to Black Power," *New York Times Magazine*, September 25, 1966, reprint in *Black Protease in the Sixties: Essays from the New York Times Magazine*, August Meier, John Bracey Jr., and Elliott Rudwick, eds. (New York: Markus Wierner Publication, 1991), 140-141; Frantz Fanon, *The Wretched on Earth* (New York: Grove 1967).

23.   Anna Karriem, "The preacher of Pan-Africanism," *Muhammad Speaks*, April 16, 1971, 15.

24.   Sister Marguerite X, Has Found Path to True Liberation, Righteousness in the nation of Islam *Muhammad Speaks*, August 29, 1969, 17.

25. Brother Preston X (Dixon), "Says Black Students Union Is Ersatz; the Nation of Islam is the Real Thing," *Muhammad Speaks*, July 25 (1969), 17.

26. Ula. Y. Taylor, J. Tarika Lewis, and Marion Van Peebles, Panther: A Pictorial History of the Black Panther Party and the Story behind the File (New York: New Market Press, 1955).

27. Huey Newton, *Revolutionary Suicide* (New York: New Market Press).

28. Charles Marsh, *God's Long Summer: Stories of Faith and Civil Rights* (Princeton, NJ: Princeton University Press, 1977), 181.

29. Brother Preston X (Dixon), "Say Black Students Union is Erastx," 17. *Muhammad Speaks*, August 29, 1969.

30. Ibid.

31. Joan 4X, "What Islam Has Done For ME," *Muhammad Speaks*, October 24, 1969, 13.

32. Ibid.

33. Joan 4X, What Islam Has Done For ME," *Muhammad Speaks*, October 24, 1969, 13.

34. *The Black Women Oral History Project: a Guide to the Transcripts* / edited by Ruth Edmonds Hill and Patricia Miller King, Cambridge, Mass.: Radcliffe College, 1989, Edition Rev.

35. Malcolm X, *February 1965: The Final Speeches*, Steve Clark, ed. (New York: Pathfinder, 1992), 205.

36. Moore Interview, 151.

37. Elijah Muhammad, *Message to the Blackman in America* (Philadelphia, Penn.: Hakim Publishing, 1965), 35.

38. Sister Christine Delois X, "Dope, Alcohol and Devils Tricks Strip Blacks of Human Dignity," *Muhammad Speaks,* January 29, 1971, 18.

39. James Baldwin. *The Price of the Ticker: Collected Nonfiction 1948-1985* (New York: St. Martin Press, 1985) 360.

40. Alvin F. Poussaint, "A Negro Psychiatrist Explains the Negro Psyche," *New York Times Magazine*, August 20, 1967, reprint in August Meier, Elliot Rudwick and John Bracey, Jr., eds., Black Protest into the Sixties Article from the *New York Times.*

41. John Kope Franklin and Alfred A. Moss, Jr, *From Slavery to Freedom: A History of African Americans* (Boston, MA: McGraw-Hill, 2000) 138.

42. David Jackson and William Gains, "Nation of Islam: Power of Money," *Chicago Tribune*, March 12, 1995, 16.

43. Brother Herbert X, Explains How Messenger Laid Out Olan for Economic Freemont in Slave Land," *Muhammad Speaks* April 21, 1967, 25

44. Brother Charles JX, "Found Solutions to All MY Problems Lay with Islam," *Muhammad Speaks*, August 29, 1969, 17.

45. Sister Beverly Maurad, "Sister Beverley Addresses All Islam Grads," *Muhammad Speaks*, March 19, 1971

46. Sonsyrea Tate, *Little X Growing Up in the Nation of Islam* (San Francisco: HarperCollins, 1997) 84.

47. Joan 4X, "What Islam Has Done For ME," *Muhammad Speaks*, October 24, 1969, 13.

48. T. H. Marshall, *Citizenship and Social Class* (Cambridge: Cambridge University Press, 1950), 29.

49. Muhammad, message to the Blackman, 59.

50. Paulette Pierce, "Boudoir Politics and the Birthing of the Nation," in *Women Out of Place: The Gender of Agene and the Race of Nationality*, Backers F. Williams, ed. (New York: Roulade, 1966)

51.   Barbara Smith, "Some Home Truths on the Contemporary Black Feminist Move-ment," in *Works of Fire: An Anthology of African Americans Feminist Thought*, Beverly Ful-Sheftall, ed. (New York: The New Press, 1985).
52.   African Congress: a Documentary of the First Modern Pan-African Congress. Edited with an introduction by Imamu Amiri Baraka (LeRoi Jones), New York: Morrow, 1972.
53.   African Congress: a Documentary of the First Modern Pan-African Congress. Edited with an introduction by Imamu Amiri Baraka (LeRoi Jones), New York: Morrow, 1972.
54.   Muhammad, *Message to the Blackman*, 60
55.   Eldridge Cleaver, *Soul on Ice*
56.   Pierce, *Boudoir Politics and the Birthing of the Nation*
57.   Sister Charles Ann X, Says Islam Lifts up the Black Women, Giving Her Wisdom Knowledge, Strength, *Muhammad Speaks*
58.   Sandra JX, Black Women Finds Peace, Freedom in Folds in Islam,
59.   Sister Mabel X," Greatest Gift She has ever known,
60.   Aaron Etta X Anderson, *Muhammad Speaks*
61.   Melba. H. X. (Walker), "Muslim Sister finds Real Meaning of Black Beauty,"
62.   Muhammad, Warning it the MGT and GC class, *Muhammad Speaks*
63.   Elijah Muhammad, Beards, *Muhammad Speaks*, July 4, 1965
64.   Marguerite X, "What Islam Had Done For Me," *Muhammad Speaks*, August 2 1968
65.   Sister Evelyn, Modest Muslim Dress Dignifies Black women
66.   Hale After, Why Fundamentalism? Iranian Women and Their Support of Islam, *Women: A Cultural Review* 6:4

2

Biography and Africology: Method and Interpretation

James L. Conyers, Jr.

Introduction

Academic and independent scholars have attempted to provide a context, framework, and deductive analysis, to describe and evaluate the term biography. In general, this concept refers to the writing and reporting on a singular life, in the second person narrative, organized within one of any four categories: (1) literary; (2) full scale; (3) political; and (4) intellectual approaches by an observer in the second person. For a survey descriptor, S.A. Adejunmobi writes about biography in the following:

> It is often stated that history is biography and biography is history, or that history is the essence of innumerable biographies. Yet, few teachers and schools consider seriously the biographical approach to the teaching of history or social studies. Simply put, biography is a written account or history of the life of an individual by another person. Thus, introducing biography into schools, its advocates contend, has many advantages. The first relates to the psychological dictum which states that since children are more interested in people and their deeds than in the wider issues of the society, history for them should be centered on lives if individuals.[1]

In addition, Barbara Laslett notes,

> Yet, in practice, little attention has been given to biography as a form of research appropriate to the interests of sociologists. In fact, if one takes the term biography literally—as the story of an individual life—it is generally seen as an inappropriate unit of sociological analysis. For inevitably the question is raised, "how can the particularities of an individual life provide a basis for theorizing about social processes in general?"[2]

Branford Smith remarks, "Biography—the word itself means life writing. And how can you write life except by imitating its characteristics qualities—unless you show people talking, loving, hating, moving about, leaving their marks on each other?"[3] Still, the process to cipher, probe, and conceptualize the writings of biography on an individual life sequesters a narrative, whereas the individual being studied is referenced as human. Admittedly, this is not rhetorical commentary, but an observation extended on the basis of acknowledging the impact of hegemony used as a tool of interpretative analysis. More to the point, this commentary and loaded query is raised to address attention toward the ideas of culture, agency, and normative values of Africana phenomena. As such, Africana people have location as humans and, moreover, the capacity to identify and locate retentions of their culture throughout the diaspora. Even more important, Marimba Ani notes:

> Traditionally, African culture is an extremely well-ordered construct, since it is informed by a world view characterized by the themes of unity and harmony, of wholeness and equilibrium. The health of the society within that context depends on the maintenance of a balance between complementary forces. When that balance is upset, for whatever reason, the order is threatened and otherwise neutral forces can become dangerous to the community.[4]

Hence, W.N. Medlicott writes about the functional value of the use of biography in historical studies, in the following manner: "Biography and the systematic demographic approach can be of great value in all fields of modern history, where the abundance of records open up possibilities of investigation denied to the documentarily-starved students of earlier centuries."[5]

Conversely, this lends engagement toward the attempt to briefly describe the term Africology. In a historical word, the Afrocentric movement had moderate vibration and advancement during the 1980s-90s. Indeed, with engagement and growth within this academic body of knowledge, so came the amenities of debate about nomenclature and existentialism. Dialogue from this query sequestered Africana studies scholars to organize and compose humanistic and social science data by developing matrices concerning theory and methods. In short, Africology refers to the study of Africana phenomena from an Afrocentric perspective. Ani provides an active voice to explain this issue, by writing:

> An understanding of our experience in North America necessitates the use of two concepts. They are *ethos* and *world view*—useful cultural concepts which refer to essential aspects of collective human experience. Ethos is intimately related to culture, both influencing it and being influenced by it. Ethos refers in part to the emotional substance of a cultural group, to their collective "emotional tone." But by using the term ethos we are accepting the idea that, when a group of people share a common heritage, a common set of experiences, and a common culture, an emotional bond is created between them.[6]

One of the outcome's assessments is the posture of cultural agency, which positions Africana phenomena as subjects and not objects. Continuing on the theme of cultural agency provides space for Africana Studies scholars to advance scientific information offering an alternative world view. Shafer discusses the added value incentive to cultural location, saying:

"We are here interested in ideas because (a) they influenced past events; (b) they influence the historian's interpretation of past events; and (c) difficult problems of proof arise in connection with the effort to show the influence of ideas in human affairs."[7]

In short, the aim and objective of this essay focuses on five areas of interest, with emphasis to biography and Africology, which are the following: (1) biography and method; (2) Africology and interpretative analysis; (3) biography and analysis; (4) Africology as a disciplinary matrix; and (5) conclusion with commentary and analysis for the use of biography as a research tool of analysis in Africological studies.

Biography and Method

As mentioned previously, I provided a general working definition for the term biography. Furthermore, the concept of research and writing of biographical studies is becoming more commonplace within social science research and writing. Some humanists and social scientists have introduced research tools of mixed methodology and metatheory. For example, the use of: psychoanalysis, existentialism, essentialism, deconstruction, political theory, and content analysis, are a few of the theoretical and methodological approaches of describing and evaluating data. James W. Anderson offers a brief explanation on this topic by noting: "Even the harshest critics of psychological biography concede that the application of psychology to biography makes sense. Since comprehensive biographical studies inevitably include an analysis of the subject's personality, it is reasonable to carry out such analysis systematically and with psychological sophistication. But, as even the fiercest proponents of psychobiography admit, psychobiographical studies tend to be reductionistic, narrow, and disparaging. A marked disparity exists between the potential and the execution of psychobiography."[8]

To probe this study further, table 1.0 is a chart which list biographical comparative studies. The table has four general areas of classification: (1) author's name; (2) title of book; (3) genre; and (4) structural organization of text. For example, some of the genres listed are: autobiography; biography (intellectual); oral history; biography (literature) and biography (political).

TABLE 1.0
Biographical Studies Comparatives

AUTHOR	TITLE OF BOOK	GENRE	STRUCTURE
William L. Andrews	*To Tell a Free Story*	Autobiography	Narratives
Jacqueline A. Goggin	*Carter G. Woodson: A Life in Black History*	Biography Intellectual	Narrative
Alex Haley	*The Autobiography of Malcolm X*	Autobiography	2nd Person Narrative
Henry Hampton & Steve Foyer	*Voices of Freedom Oral History*	Oral History	Narratives
David L. Lewis	*King: A Biography*	Biography	Intellectual
Manning Marable	*W.E.B. DuBois: Black Radical Democrat*	Political Biography	Conceptual
Nell I. Painter	*Sojourner Truth: A Life A Symbol Biography*	Biography	Intellectual
Arnold Rampersad	*The Art and Imagination of W.E.B. DuBois*	Biography Literary	Narrative
Julius Thompson	*Dudley Randall, Broadside Press, Black Art Movement in Detroit 1960-1995*	Biography Literary	Narrative

Ken Lawrence writes:

The most massive and complete product of these early oral history collections is *The American Slave: A Composite Autobiography* by George P. Rawick. SO far nineteen volumes have appeared, and more are expected. Sixteen of these contain the Federal Writers' Project Slave Narratives and two are reprints of the Fisk University collections, *Unwritten History Slavery* and *God Struck Me Dead*.

Rawick's introductory volume, *From Sundown to Sunup: the Making of the Black Community*, has been called "the most valuable book I know of by a white man about slave life in the United States," by Eugene D. Genovese, himself a prominent historian of slavery. It is a challenge to almost all previous histories that were based primarily on accounts of slavery written by slaveholders and journalists.

Rawick says that historians have been aware of the existence of slave autobiographies and narratives for a long time. But in almost every case white historians have chosen to believe the account of white oppressors or casual observers, rather than to rely on slaves' descriptions of their own lives.[9]

The purpose of presenting this information in table 1.0 is to outline a contextual boundary for scholars in Africana Studies to organize research and writing centered within biographical or closely related subject areas. In fact, when conducting research within any of these subject areas, researchers will often find themselves borrowing or using tools from studies located within the boundaries of autobiography, oral history, and political biography. Gould P. Colman asserts:

> A good oral history memoir demands, on the part of the interviewer, thoroughgoing research on subjects he expects to raise during each interview and, equally important, a continuing analysis of how the content of the interview may have been affected by his relations with the person he is interviewing.[10]

Jan Vansina reports:

> Oral traditions consist of all verbal testimonies which are reported statements concerning the past. This definition implies that nothing but *oral* traditions—that is to say, statements either spoken or sung—enter into consideration. These must not only be distinguished from written statements, but also from material objects that might be used as a source of knowledge about the past.[11]

For example, Alex Haley writes about the intersection of black history, oral history and genealogy, in the following manner:

> When I was a little boy I lived in a little town which you probably never heard of called Henning, Tennessee, about 50 miles north of Memphis. And I lived there with my parents in the home of my mother's mother. And my grandmother and I were very, very close. Every summer that I can remember growing up there in Henning, my grandmother would have, as visitors, members of the family who were always women, always of her general age range, the late forties, early fifties. They came from places that sounded pretty exotic to me—Dyersburg, Tennessee; Inkster, Michigan—places like that, St. Louis, Kansas City. They were like Cousin Georgia, Aunt Pius, Aunt Liz, so forth. And every evening, after the supper dishes were washed, they would go out on the front porch and sit in cane-bottomed rocking chairs, and I would always sit behind grandma's chair. And every single evening of those summers, unless there was some particularly hot gossip that would overrule it, they would talk about otherwise the self same thing. It was bits and pieces and patches of what I later would learn was a long narrative history of the family which had been passed down literally across generations.[12]

Oral history research is also a test of ourselves, of our ability to deserve and win the confidence of other people, of our ability to deal sympathetically but honestly and imaginatively with their memories, and of our ability to deal honestly with ourselves. All these tests are involved also, if not always so obviously, in more traditional historical research. Oral history is therefore good training for other kinds of history and may be a path to a greater understanding of ourselves and others, including not only those alive now but also those who have ceased to live except in our imaginations.[13] Jan Vansina asserts:

Ethnologists who have attempted to study the past of peoples without writing have been faced with the problem of how much worth to attach to oral tradition. Hence a number of them have devoted a certain amount of attention to the problem. The following are the six main attitudes adopted:

1.   Oral traditions are never reliable.

2.   Oral traditions may contain a certain amount of truth.

3.   It is impossible to assess the amount of truth contained in oral tradition.

4.   All oral traditions contain a kernel of historical truth.

5.   All factors affecting the reliability of traditions should be thoroughly examined.

6.   The reliability of these sources should be examined according to the usual canons of historical methodolog.[14]

Figure 1.1
Africology and Interpretive Analysis

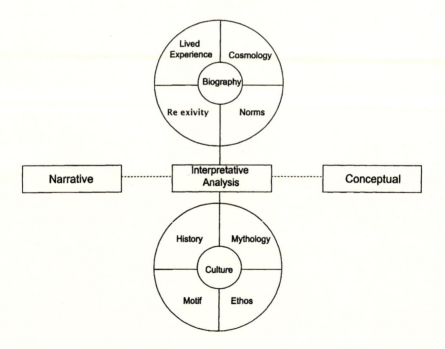

Figure 1.1 is a descriptive charting of biography, which cites an interpretative analysis of: lived experiences (historical and cultural memory); reflexivity (past, present, and contemporary issues); norms (values and mores); and cosmology (worldview). Moreover, there are two general schema that focus on: (1) narrative; and (2) conceptual studies. Additionally, within the process of narrative studies, one engages, theory or the use of metatheory. As in the case of conceptual studies, a researcher may find more use of social science approaches of collecting data, to fuse the employment of theory and research methods.

Still, with the use of narrative and conceptual tools, one can dismiss or lose focus of the humanistic and social science purpose of biography. Robert J. Shafer advances:

> History shares with the social and behavioral sciences the problem of grappling with highly intractable subject matter. Large-scale human activity involves huge numbers of interlocking variables. Observation of human activity, either directly or indirectly by means of little glimpses in documents or artifacts, is imprecise. Experiments cannot be set up to control the environment or reduce the number of variables to manageable proportions.[15]

In sum, the objective is not to recount the life of the subject, but to explain, enumerate, and offer how the subject related their ideas and thoughts to common people, which can be evaluated in place, space, and time. In this way, perhaps, readers can borrow tools and ideas from a singular life for the advancement of: humanism, policy, education, technology, and science. In an ambidextrous manner, Smith provides a philosophical outline concerning the role and mission of the biographer, writing:

> The biographer is a queer duck. Neither historian nor novelist, he tries to be both. He uses the techniques of the historian to get his man and get him right, yet he must use the art of the novelist to bring him back alive. For he will not be worth bringing if he comes stuffed. The biographer is a hunter, not a taxidermist. No one would buy a circus ticket to see a stuffed lion. No one wants to read a biography that is stuffed with scholarship rather than with blood, brains and guts. So the biographer is in a ticklish position from the start. He has to appeal to a general audience—to people who want at least to be kept awake, if not lifted out of their seats.[16]

Though my perspective and analysis are limited to an alternative viewpoint, an integral element is that biography, much like other genres and bodies of knowledge, is to assist us in our perceptions, views, and forethought concerning society on a national and international tier. John Henrik Clarke writes:

In "Racial Historical Societies and the American Tradition," included in his book, *Neglected History* (1965), the Afro-American historian, Charles H. Wesley, describes the work of ethnic historical societies in this manner: "They must gather up precious records and interpret them. Both in language and in that subtle understanding which they have absorbed by natural circumstances of the way of life of their own folk, they possess keys to unlock doors that bar the way to a full comprehension of the social history of America."[17]

Clearly phrased, the use of this research tool can augment and assist to contribute to the body of knowledge and information in the discipline of Africology. Moreover, Adejunmobi discusses issues relevant of method by writing:

It is not uncommon to discover that in most societies what determines greatness is sometimes the sheer whims of fortune which may be manipulated by the great man himself, or by others who record events in order to please the powers that be. That is why we find that sometimes a man may be denied greatness by one age and accorded it by another. It is also true that greatness is usually associated with relative and variable from one age to another. One might also ask whether fame comes only to people who embody the characteristics of their own generation, or those who do not.[18]

On the other hand, Jo Burr Margadant discusses the use of biographical methodology as:

Pierre Nora challenged several mandarins of the French historical profession ... revealed through two decades of historiographical debate by writing a new kind of life and times biography called ego-histoire.... History in ego-histoire becomes a script, historians become actors, and everyone becomes a spectator to the deconstruction of the theater of power which practitioners of objective historical investigation had fashioned with themselves offstage.[19]

However, within a Matrix of Africology, there is concern that scholars and writers of Africana biography dismiss or abort the variables of culture. Yet, within examining works of continental African culture, the idea of studying a subject in isolation of their families and communities would be perceived as ineffective and disconnects this life to have substance and graciousness of a collective. John D. Hargreaves writes about this dilemma in the following:

Biographical works of African interest continue to appear; and it is proper that they should be approached and criticised, not merely for their general interest and literary value, but as contributions to a historical problem of contemporary concern. The writers of such biographies often face peculiarly difficult problems of documentation. The physical conditions of African life, at the time of the scramble and since, have often impeded the orderly filing or correspondence and its subsequent preservation.[20]

In the previous citations mentioned, I offered a survey approach to the function and use of biographical studies. However, with a sense of agency and cultural grounding, the use of biography in Africana Studies is flexible. This concept of elasticity is functional and allows scholars in the discipline of Africology the opportunity to apply various tools of analysis from the genre of biography in the process of describing and evaluating the Africana experience. Whereas, to study African people as subjects and having humanism, can in many ways provide an alternative worldview. James Baldwin states:

> The argument concerning the use, or the status, or the reality, Black English is rooted in American history and has absolutely nothing to do with the question the argument supposes itself to be posing. The argument has nothing to do with the language itself but with the role of language. Language, incontestably, reveals the speaker. Language, also, far more dubiously, is meant to define the other—and, in this case, the other is refusing to be defined by a language that has never been able to recognize him.... What joins all languages, and all men, is the necessity to confront life, in order, not inconceivably, to outwit death: The price for this is the acceptance, and achievement, of one's temporal identity. [21]

Not to offer a bland or sketchy commentary, the point made is that people of African decent consistently have to write themselves into history as humans.

Biography and Analysis

The process of writing a second person narrative-conceptual study takes on a number of perspectives and approaches. With emphasis on analysis, the task then incorporates concepts such as culture and worldview, to describe and evaluate Africana phenomena. Nevertheless, within a theoretical framework of biography and analysis, within an interdisciplinary matrix of Africana, Richard W. Brislin continues to discuss this categorization of research, by mentioning the role of comparative research methodology in cross-cultural studies. He adds:

> The potential contributions of cross-cultural psychology to theory development (and the approach will ultimately rise or fall on the basis of its contribution to theory) have been discussed in several places (Strodtbeck, 1964); will be emphasized here: (1) Cross-cultural psychology can extend the range of independent variables beyond that found in any one culture. "Range" can include clearly operational zed definitions involving ratio scales, such as average age of weaning (which can occur as late as age five, an average age far later than in the United States or Western Europe); or, the extract content of independent variables in various cultures, such as the nature of in group vs. out-group membership or the nature of the need for achievement. (2) Cross-cultural psychology can make theory more precise by identifying cultures in which people, at first examination, seem to elicit behavior not in line with a certain theory developed from observation in one line country. For instance, the cross-cultural work using Piagetian tasks (reviewed by Dasen, 1972) forced developers of Piagetian theory to place more emphasis on childhood experience that could affect the ages at which various stages of performance on conversation task are reached (see Piaget, 1966).[22]

G. R. Elton writes:

> ... political history is the study of that dynamic activity in the past experience of human societies which has direct relevance to the organizational aspects of those societies. That is to say, it is concerned with those activities which arise from the fact that men create, maintain, transform, and destroy social structures in which they live.

Elton continues:

> The subject matter of political history is, therefore, that agglomerate of "affairs" which at one time constituted in effect the whole content of written history. Nowadays, the questions we ask of the past have proliferated; we want to know not only what men did in public life, but how they lived (social history), how they organized wealth (economic history), what and how they thought (intellectual history), how they expressed their sense of beauty (history of art), and so on.[23]

On the other hand, Ama Mazama contends there are central and numerous problems which conform alternative paradigms and perspectives. She notes:

> Afrocentricity contends that our main problem as African people is our usually unconscious adoption of the Western worldview and perspective and their attendant conceptual frameworks. The list of those ideas and theories that have invaded our lives as normal, natural, or even worse, ideal is infinite. How many of us have really paused to seriously examine and challenge such ideas as development, planning, progress, the need for democracy and the nation-state as the best form of political and social organization, to name only a few?[24]

For example, DuBois uses the monograph series at Atlanta University, a variable to exhibit the relevance and rationale of culture in the way of interpreting data. Elliott Rudwick notes:

> In spite of the shortcomings to the Atlanta studies, what actual merit did those possess for science and society? If Du Bois must be held to his early goal of science, i.e., the ability of measuring the extent of prejudice in causing the Negro problem. As differentiated from the Negroes' own cultural shortcomings, his contributions are small. However, other American social scientists were hardly more successful in understanding our prejudice. The truth is that Du Bois's Atlanta studies represent his efforts to introduce systematic induction into the field of take relations, when other men were speculating about the Negro.[25]

Ayele Berkerie defines the general survey approach to Afrocentric theory as:

> ...when is an Afrocentric theory? Afro centric theory is a theory that recognizes the need to look at Africa's cultures and history from their own centers of locations. It is a proposition to validate, regenerate, create, and perpetuate African life and living whole and unhindered, informed by African perspective or world outlook. In short, as Asante (1990) puts it, the theory posits that African peoples are active, primary, and central agents in the making of their histories (p.5). This is the guiding principle under which scholars of the Temple Schools, such as Asante, C. T. Keto, Kariamu Welsh-Asante, Abu Abarry, Ella Forbes, Nilgum Okur, Ama Mazama, Terry Kershaw, and more than 200 graduate students conduct their studies and research.

Afrocentricity, as an intellectual enterprise, seems to have become a catalyst in the often heated but lively debate among a wide range of thinkers and scholars with respect to the production and use of knowledge, particularly what Kershaw calls emancipator knowledge.[26]

Africology and Interpretation

As noted in Figure 1.2, there are approaches to the organizational structure of this academic enterprise and holistic research methodologies. The sphere of culture provides the centerpiece for describing and evaluating phenomena. Continuing on, the variable of interpretation solicits the germ seed and window to engage the topic of discusion.

Figure 1.2
Africology Disciplinary Matrix

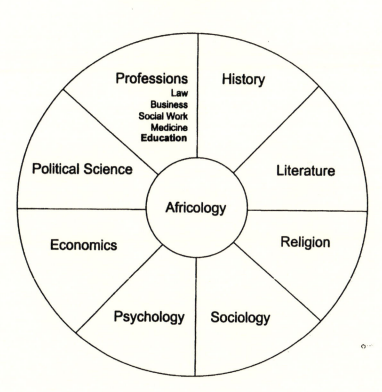

Diagram 1.2 is a general operating explanation of examining two spheres and three quadrilaterals. The two spheres are:

1. Conceptual approach to examining biography, with the descriptive variables of: (a) reflexivity; (b) lived experience; (c) cosmology; and (d) norms.
2. The sphere represents four survey attributes of culture, which refer to: history, mythology, motif, and ethos.

In summary, the diagram represents an alternative approach to discussing an Interpretive Analysis. Equally important, the three quadrilaterals represent: (1) narrative; (2) interpretative analysis; and (3) conceptual organizational approaches to conducting biographical studies within the disciplinary matrix of African Studies.

Conclusion

The general purpose of this essay was to offer dialog, diagrams, and context, with an emphasis on conducting biographical studies, from an interdisciplinary perspective. Furthermore, the term interdisciplinary perspective, directly and indirectly, provides a correlation to the linguistic components of Africana Studies. Smitherman diagrams a literary canon to describe and evaluate Africana linguistics, by writing:

> I discuss the following patterns of USEB: (1) aspectual *be*; (2) stressed *been*; (3) multiple negation; (4) adjacency/context in possessives; (5) postvocalic /r/ deletion; (6) copula absence; (7) camouflaged and other unique lexical forms.[27]

Grounded within theory and methods, there is the attempt to exhaust and utilize data, which examines the lived experiences of Africana phenomena on a national and international basis. Still, the use of sources, meta-theory, and mixed methodology, provide a framework, which extends beyond conventional studies conducted within the social sciences and humanities. Geneva Smitherman notes:

> The above are only some of the patterns in the grammatical, phonological, and semantic systems of USEB. To explore the full 360 degrees of USEB, we need to move on to styles of speaking. In fact, it is the area of communicative practices—rhetorical strategies and modes of discourse—that cuts across gender, generation, and class in the African-American community. USEB speech acts may be classified as follows: (1) Call-Response; (2) Total Semantics; (3) Narrativizing; (4) Proverb Use/Proverbializing; (5) Significant/Signifyin; (6) The Dozens/Snappin/Joanin. Discussion of two of these discourse modes follows.[28]

Perhaps, scholars might consider alternative queries and variables to raise and examine when conducting community, biographical, oral history, and autobiographical studies. Nevertheless, the exercise of presenting fresh perspectives can possibly lend to a body of knowledge centered on enhancement, rather than replication of existing sources and information.

Notes

1. S.A. Adejunmobi, "The Biographical Approach to the Teaching of History," The History Teacher, Volume 12, Issue 3, (May, 1979), pp. 349-357 (page 349).
2. Barabara Laslett, "Biography as Historical Sociology: The Case of William Fielding Ogburn," Theory and Society, Volume 20, Issue 4, (August 1991), 511-538, (511).
3. Branford Smith, "Biographer=s Creed," The William and Mary Quarterly, Third Series, Volume 10, Issue 2 (April 1953), pp. 190-195, (191).
4. Marimba Ani, aka Dona Richards, "The Implications of African American Spirituality," p. 208, in African Culture: The Rhythms of Unity, Molefi Kete Asante and Kariamu Welsh Asante, eds.,Westport, CT: Greenwood Press, 1985.
5. W.N. Medlicott, "Contemporary History in Biography," Journal of Contemporary History, Volume 7, Issue 2 (January-April, 1972), pp. 91-106, (91).
6. Marimba Ani, aka Dona Richards, "The Implications of African American Spirituality," p. 227, in African Culture: The Rhythms of Unity, Molefi Kete Asante and Kariamu Welsh Asante, eds.,Westport, CT: Greenwood Press, 1985.
7. Robert Jones Shafer, A Guide to Historical Method, Homewood, IL: The Dorsey Press, 1969, p. 19.
8. James William Anderson, "The Methodology of Psychological Biography," Journal of Interdisciplinary History, Volume 11, Issue 3 (Winter, 1981), pp. 455-475, (455).
9. Ken Lawrence, "Oral History of Slavery," Southern Exposure 1, nos. 3 and 4: 84-86, p. 84.
10. Gould P. Colman, "Oral History—An Appeal for More Systematic Procedures," American Archivist 28 (January 1965): 79-83, p.82.
11. Jan Vansina, Oral Tradition: A Study in Historical Methodology, Chicago: Aldine Publishing Company, 1965, p. 19.
12. Alex Haley, "Black History, Oral History and Geneology," Oral History Review, 1973, pp. 1-25, p. 1.
13. James Hoopes, Oral History, Chapel Hill, NC: University of North Carolina Press, 1979, p. 5.
14. Jan Vanisna, Oral Tradition: A Study in Historical Methodology, Chicago: Aldine Publishing Company, 1965, p. 8.
15. Robert Jones Shafer, A Guide to Historical Method, Homewood, IL: The Dorsey Press, 1969, p. 5.
16. Branford Smith, "Biographer's Creed," The William and Mary Quarterly, Third Series, Volume 10, Issue 2 (April 1953), pp. 190-195, (190).
17. John Henrik Clark, "African American Historians and the Reclaiming of African History," p. 165 in African Culture: The Rhythms of Unity, Molefi Kete Asante and Kariamu Welsh Asante, eds., Westport, CT: Greenwood Press, 1985.
18. Adejunmobi, p. 350.
19. Jo Burr Margadant, "Introduction: The New Biography in Historical Practice," French Historical Studies, Volume 19, Issue 4, Special Issue: Biography (Autumn, 1996), 1045-1058, (page 1045).
20. John D. Hargreaves, "Biography and the Debate About Imperialism," The Journal of Modern African Studies, Volume 2, Issue 2 (July 1964), pp. 279-285, (page 280).
21. James Baldwin, "IF Black English Isn't a Language, Then Tell Me, What is?" p. 67 in The Real Ebonics Debate, Theresa Perry and Lisa Delpit, eds., Boston: Beacon Press, 1998.

22.   Richard W. Brislin, "Comparative Research Methodology: Cross Cultural Studies," International Journal of Psychology, 1976, Vol. II, No. 3, pp. 215 229.

23.   G. R. Elton, Political History: Principles and Practice, New York: Basic Books, 1970, p. 3.

24.   Ama Mazama, "The Afrocentric Paradigm; Contours and Definition." Journal of Black Studies, vol. 31, No. 4 (Mar. 2001) pp. 387. 387 405.

25.   Elliott M. Rudwick, "W.E.B. Du Bois and the Atlanta University Studies on the Negro," The Journal of Negro Education, vol. 26, No. 4 (autumn 1957) pp. 466 476.

26.   Ayele Bekerie," The Four Corners of a Circle; Afro Centricity as a Model of Syntheses," Journal of Black Studies, Vol.25, No.2 (Dec. 1994), pp. 131-149.

27.   Geneva Smitherman, "Black English/Ebonics: What It Be Like?" p. 31, in The Real Ebonics Debate, Theresa Perry and Lisa Delpit, eds., Boston: Beacon Press, 1998.

3

Africana Studies and the Quest for Black Economic Empowerment: What Can Be Done?

Robert E. Weems, Jr.

Since its inception in the late 1960s, the discipline of Africana/Black Studies, as an offshoot of the Black Power Movement, has been credited with enhancing the psyche and self-worth of persons of African descent. For instance, blacks' evolution from "Negroes" to "African-Americans" clearly validates this assertion. Nevertheless, while persons of African descent, in recent decades, have demonstrated their appreciation of cultural integrity, there has not been a similar demonstration of interest in Africana economic integrity. In fact, since the late 1960s, there has been an accelerated decline and disappearance of such historic institutions as black-owned insurance companies. Thus, it appears that one of the major challenges facing Africana Studies in the twenty-first century is to be in the vanguard of a movement to redemonstrate (to blacks) the merits of economic integrity and cooperation.

Despite its many accomplishments (including serving as a stimulus for the establishment of Africana Studies Departments/Programs), one of the major deficiencies of the Black Power Movement was its lack of a credible "game plan" for black economic empowerment. Although the Black Power Movement ostensibly placed a special emphasis upon insular African-American economic development (Van Deburg 116-120, Walker 271-272), persons like Stokely Carmichael ("Kwame Ture"), H. Rap Brown, and other visible Black Power advocates had never started and maintained a business enterprise. Consequently, the input and expertise of older black businesspeople could have benefited the Black Power Movement. Unfortunately, since much of the Black Power Movement focused upon such external considerations as wearing Afros and dashikis, many older black businessmen, who kept their hair short and continued to wear traditional business suits, were often labeled as "Uncle Toms." In retrospect, this condemnation of established black businessmen appears to have been a serious error. Without the active input and expertise of persons who had spent their professional lives providing goods and services to the African-American community, the militant Black Power Movement's call for community economic development never developed into anything more than mere rhetoric (Weems 156).

Besides their failure to comply with the external ambiance of the Black Power Movement, the evidence suggests that traditional black business-people were shunned and scorned during the late 1960s and early 1970s for two other distinct reasons. First, a noteworthy body of scholarship depicting black businesspeople as "villains" attracted a large readership during this period. Second, President Richard M. Nixon's promotion of his "Black Capitalism" initiative raised the proverbial "red flag" in many sectors of Black America (based upon widely-held African-American perceptions of Nixon as "Tricky Dick").

Earl Ofari's widely-discussed 1970 book *The Myth of Black Capitalism* represented, perhaps, the period's most strident denunciation of black businesspeople. The following introductory quotes succinctly set the stage for this work: (Ofari 3)

> You show me a capitalist, I'll show you a bloodsucker. He cannot be anything but a bloodsucker if he's going to be a capitalist. He's got to get it from somewhere other than himself, and that's where he gets it—from somewhere or someone other than himself.—Malcolm X

> As long as the Man controls the water or electricity coming into your community, it does you no good to control that community. And to control the community in a capitalistic way, like the Man, is not desirable.—H. Rap Brown

> The mode of production in material life determines the general character of the social, political, and spiritual processes of life.—Karl Marx

Ofari, using E. Franklin Frazier's controversial 1957 study *Black Bourgeoisie* as a reference point, asserted, among other things, that contemporary interest in black business development came primarily from the black middle and upper classes (Ofari 10). Significantly, by directly associating black business with a nefarious, self-interested, "black elite," Ofari exhibited a stunning unfamiliarity with census data related to black-owned businesses in America. Historically, most black-owned businesses have been single proprietorships operated by African-Americans from a variety of economic backgrounds (Hall 496-498, *Survey of Minority-Owned Business-Black* 9-10). Nevertheless, despite its analytical and methodological flaws, *The Myth of Black Capitalism* influenced the thinking of some blacks during this period.

Richard Nixon's promotion of "Black Capitalism" during his first Presidential Administration also appears to have helped generate a negative perception of business development among some African-Americans (during the Black Power era). As political scientist Lewis A. Randolph and I demonstrated in our 2001 article, "The Ideological Origins of Richard M. Nixon's 'Black Capitalism' Initiative," Nixon's interest in black business development represented one manifestation of his pronounced "Machiavellian" political instincts.

Candidate and later President Richard M. Nixon viewed an uncontrolled Black Power Movement as a major threat to the internal security of the United States (during the late 1960s and early 1970s). To address this situation, Nixon developed his "Black Capitalism" initiative as a domestic version of his widely-publicized foreign policy initiative of "detente" (which sought to "contain" the power of the Soviet Union and China). Significantly, just as Nixon and his Secretary of State Henry Kissinger linked concessions associated with "detente" to Soviet and Chinese behavior modification, the Nixon Presidency offered African-Americans the notion of "Black Capitalism" as an incentive to repudiate the nihilistic notion of "Burn Baby Burn" and the more thoughtful (Marxist-influenced) notion of "Power to the People" (Weems, Randolph 53-58).

While contemporary African-Americans were, indeed, justified in their suspicions of Richard M. Nixon, some blacks' subsequent distrust and disinterest in black business development (because Nixon publicly supported African-American entrepreneurship) has had some disturbing consequences. Again, it is more than ironic that the past thirty-five to forty years have witnessed both a simultaneous increase in African-American cultural pride and spending power and the increasing disappearance of historic black-owned enterprises from the landscape of American business. The recent history of the black-owned insurance industry provides a chilling example of this contradictory situation.

African-American insurance companies, historically, had been the cornerstone of black economic development. Evolving from a tradition of mutual aid, dating back to Philadelphia's Free African Society founded in 1787, black-owned insurance companies have attempted to perpetuate economic and social cooperation among African-Americans. Yet, despite their historic importance, African-American insurance companies, since the1960s, have engaged in an increasingly difficult struggle for survival.

In my Fall 1994 essay, "A Crumbling Legacy: The Decline of African American Insurance Companies in Contemporary America" (which appeared in *The Review of Black Political Economy*), I discussed the trials and tribulations of modern black insurers.

Between 1962-1992, the number of African-American insurers dropped from fifty to twenty-three, a 54 percent decrease. For the industry as a whole, the number of firms grew by 35.5 percent (1,479 to 2,005) (Weems 29). Similarly, an examination of black insurance companies' total assets and premium income, relative to the larger insurance industry, further corroborated the relative decline of African-American insurers between 1962-1992. During this period, the increase in black insurance companies' total assets and premium income trailed far behind similar figures for the industry at large.

In 1962, the total assets of the top fifteen African-American insurance companies stood at $303 million. By 1992, the total assets of the top fifteen black insurers had risen to $711 million. Still, figures for the entire U.S. life insurance industry made these black gains appear extremely minuscule, if not irrelevant. In 1962, all life insurance firms owned admitted assets valued at $133 billion. By 1992, the total assets of U.S. life insurance companies stood at over $1.6 trillion. Thus, while African-American insurers' total assets represented 0.23 percent of all U.S. life insurance assets in 1962, this percentage dwindled to 0.05 by 1992 (Weems 30). Moreover, this data clearly indicates that the recent decline of African-American insurers took place during a boon period for the industry as a whole.

Between the years 1962-1992, the increase in black insurers' premium income also lagged far behind similar figures for the industry at large. In 1962, the top fifteen African-American insurance companies received $71 million in premium income. Thirty years later, the top fifteen black insurers collected $159 million. On the other hand, in 1962, all U.S. life insurance companies received $19 billion in premium income. Thirty years later, this figure had risen to $282 billion. Once again, an obvious discrepancy existed between black insurers' premium income increase (over time) and that of the industry as a whole. Whereas the premium income of African-American insurance companies grew by 124 percent between 1962-1992, the premium income of all U.S. life insurance companies increased by 1,385 percent. (Weems 30)

Data from the authoritative insurance industry publication *Best's Review*, for the years 1979-1992 (in the aftermath of the Black Power Movement), further depicted black insurers' shrinking premium income.

In 1979, *Best*'s listing of the top 500 U.S. and Canadian insurance companies, in terms of premium income, included the (then) top six African-American insurance companies. Yet, by 1992, only North Carolina Mutual, America's largest black insurer, remained in the *Best*'s listing. Moreover, between 1979-1992, North Carolina Mutual's rank dropped from 204 to 416 (Weems 30-33).

Since African-American insurance companies, since the 1960s, have experienced an absolute decline in their number, along with a relative decline in total assets and premium income, it should not be surprising that these firms, in recent years, have experienced significant staff reductions. As I noted in "A Crumbling Legacy," between 1982-1992, the number of persons employed by the top fifteen black insurers declined by 48.5 percent (6,106 to 3,144). During the same period, the number of persons employed by all U.S. life insurance companies grew by 23.7 percent (1,723,200 to 2,132,200) (Weems 31,34).

A later unpublished study, conducted by the author, of the top ten African-American insurance companies, between 1992-1996, revealed continued stagnation and decline relative to the larger industry. A comparative reexamination of total assets and premium income graphically illustrated this situation.

Between the years 1992-1996, the total assets of the top ten African-American insurance companies declined from $689.6 million to $680 million (*Black Enterprise* 151, 203). Conversely, during the same period, the admitted assets of all U.S. life insurance companies increased from $1.6 trillion to $2.3 trillion (*1994 Life Insurance* 5, *1997 Life Insurance* 100).

In terms of premium income, the top ten African-American insurers collected $154 million dollars in 1992. Their 1996 premium income receipts were $150.1 million, representing a 3.0 percent decrease (*Black Enterprise* 151, Brown 203). Yet, among all U.S. life insurance companies, premium income grew from $282 billion to $354 billion between 1992-1996, a 21 percent increase (*1994 Life Insurance* 5, *1997 Life Insurance* 37). Moreover, North Carolina Mutual's (NCM) continuing slide in the *Best's Review* ranking of the top 500 companies in regards to premium income, offered, yet, another sobering reminder of the black insurance industry's increasingly marginal position. NCM, America's largest black insurer, dropped from 416 to 454 between 1992-1996 (*Best's Review* 17, 31).

Black insurers' extremely tenuous position, since the 1960s, is further highlighted by recent coverage given them by *Black Enterprise*. For instance, the magazine's June, 1995 issue, which featured its annual overview of black business in America, presented a stark assessment of African-American insurance companies' role in the U.S. economy. Citing an industry analyst, *Black Enterprise* reported:

> The source who requested not to be named, says that insurance companies owned by African Americans don't compete on any level with white-owned insurance companies. Instead they issue life insurance policies, not for investment purposes, but to cover the costs associated with internment (Mack 161).

The June, 1996 issue of *Black Enterprise* was even more blunt in its observations regarding black insurers. Although it noted that the four leading African-American companies, North Carolina Mutual, Atlanta Life, Golden State Mutual, and Universal Life, would "remain viable entities in the near future," *Black Enterprise* went on to declare:

> The nation's remaining 18 black-owned insurance providers should consider merging with one another to increase their assets and customer base, so they can diversify their services, save on economies of scale and compete for market share. As it stands now, many of these firms have assets below $4 million. (Scott 164)

Although the June, 1996 *Black Enterprise* offered faint praise to the top four black insurers, its overall assessment of the black insurance industry remained bleak. After noting that the top ten African-American insurance companies collected $160 million in premium income in 1995, *Black Enterprise* asserted: "these numbers hardly compete with mainstream firms." Moreover, the magazine concluded:

> As long predicted by industry analysts, including the **BE** board of economists, the retrenchment of black-owned firms in the insurance industry will continue until these companies find ways to make their services essential to people's lives—not just their deaths. (Scott 164)

The June, 1998 *Black Enterprise* overview of the black insurance industry, perhaps motivated by North Carolina Mutual's 100th Anniversary, tried to present an upbeat portrayal of African-American insurers. Nevertheless, after surveying how North Carolina Mutual and its two chief competitors (Atlanta Life and Golden State Mutual) were managing to survive in an increasingly competitive marketplace, pessimism, predictably, crept into the analysis.

Besides the decline (and disappearance) of individual black insurance companies in recent years, the industry's trade association, the National Insurance Association, has become a sickly shadow of its former self. The June, 1998 *Black Enterprise* revealed that the NIA, which had more than forty members during the 1960s, is down to thirteen associate companies

(McCoy). Moreover, the future looks bleak for this historic African-American organization (and its affiliates). As NIA president, Larkin Teasley (the CEO of Golden State Mutual) told *Black Enterprise*:

> In my personal opinion—not that of the NIA president—I believe that in 10 years only five African American-owned insurance firms will remain. The rest will have either died or been merged with other NIA members. As for the NIA itself, perhaps it will be a memory. (McCoy 187)

The June, 1999 issue of *Black Enterprise* continued the magazine's long-standing gloomy assessment of African-American insurance companies. The author of the "B.E. Insurance Overview" noted: "The past decade has been a virtual bloodbath: the number of black-owned insurers has declined by roughly 68%, from 31 on the 1989 **BE INSURANCE COMPANIES** list to 10 on this year's ranking" (Jones 216).

America's remaining black-owned insurance companies, according to various sources, have been all but abandoned by black consumers. For example, between the years 1996-2001, African-Americans spent $38 billion on insurance. Yet, during the same period, the premium income of the top ten black insurance companies was a relatively paltry $899.1 million. Put another way, only 2.3 percent of the money contemporary African-Americans spend on insurance is spent with black-owned firms. (Weems 253).

Based upon the data, today's African-American insurance industry (sadly) appears to be beyond resuscitation. Nevertheless, if contemporary African-Americans are, indeed, interested in maintaining any sense of economic integrity, Africana Studies could be in the forefront of such a movement. Specifically, Africana/Black Studies Departments and Programs can help re-acquaint their students and the larger community with the African tradition of "rotating credit associations."

The "rotating credit association" (referred to as the "esusu" by the Yoruba) has been defined as:

> ...an association formed by a core of participants who agree to make regular contributions to a fund which is given, in whole or in part, to each contributor in rotation.... In many parts of the non-Western world, this type of association serves or has served many of the functions of Western banks. (Weems 97)

In the United States, the Chinese and Japanese communities, historically, have experienced the most success in implementing rotating credit associations. Called "hui" by the Chinese and "ko" by the Japanese, prospective Asian entrepreneurs used "hui" or "ko" to circumvent the discriminatory lending practices of white American financial institutions

(Weems 97). Moreover, the Koreans' use of the rotating credit association has helped them establish a formidable business presence in black communities since the 1970s.

The following scenario illustrates how a rotating credit association would work in the "real world." Suppose there is a group of fifty African-Americans who want to establish an "esusu" whereby each individual agrees to pay $25 a week into the collective pool for fifty weeks. The total worth of this "esusu" is $62,500. The members of the "esusu" could disburse this sum in a variety of ways. First, the members may decide to pay each member a lump sum of $1250 on a rotating (weekly) basis during the life of the "esusu" ($1250 X 50 = $62,500). Second, members of the "esusu" may decide not to take their weekly individual shares. This would provide these individuals with $62,500 to collectively invest in a particular project. Lastly, the members of an "esusu" may decide to take a portion of their individual weekly shares and invest the rest in a group project (Weems 98).

It should be noted that the above scenario represents just one "esusu" cycle. Ideally, members of an "esusu" will continue their special relationship on an ongoing basis. Tables 1, 2, and 3 illustrate how the "esusu" would work for African-Americans from a variety of economic backgrounds.

Perhaps, the ideal vehicle to promote the "esusu" concept within the African-American community is through the family. In recent years, large-scale family reunions have proliferated among blacks. If families used these gatherings to discuss establishing an "esusu," this could represent a giant step in the right direction. Moreover, other groups that share a communal bond, such as churches and fraternal organizations, also appear to be ideal places to establish an "esusu" (Weems 99).

In sum, Africana/Black Studies, over the years, has promoted scholarship and community-based programs that have helped liberate African-Americans psychologically. At this crucial juncture in history, it appears both fitting and proper that Africana/Black Studies be in the forefront of a movement to promote an African-centered concept (the "esusu') with the potential to help liberate African-Americans economically.

Table 1
The African-American "Esusu"*

$10, $25, $50, $100 Weekly Payments
50 Members

	Number of Weeks	Number of Weekly Shares Disbursed	Lump Sum Amount	Total Pool
$10	50	1	$ 500	$ 25,000
$25	50	1	1,250	62,500
$50	50	1	2,500	125,000
$100	50	1	5,000	250,000

*The number of weeks listed, along with the number of members, are arbitrary figures for the purpose of illustration. The life cycle of an "esusu" can be less than fifty weeks. Moreover, the number of "esusu" members can be less than fifty. Flexibility is one of the strengths of the "esusu."

Table 2
The African-American "Esusu"

$10, $25, $50, $100 Weekly Payments
100 Members

	Number of Weeks	Number of Weekly Shares Disbursed	Lump Sum Amount	Total Pool
$10	50	2	$ 500	$ 50,000
$25	50	2	1,250	125,000
$5	50	2	2,500	250,000
$100	50	2	5,000	500,000

Table 3
The African American "Esusu"

$10, $25, $50, $100 Weekly Payments
500 Members

	Number of Weeks	Number of Weekly Shares Disbursed	Lump Sum Amount	Total Pool
$10	50	10	$ 500	$ 250,000
$25	50	10	1,250	625,000
$50	50	10	2,500	1,250,000
$100	50	10	5,000	2,500,000

References

1994 Life Insurance Fact Book. Washington, DC: American Council of Life Insurance, 1994.

1997 Life Insurance Fact Book Update. Washington, DC: American Council of Life Insurance, 1997.

"A New Day for Black Financial Institutions?" *Black Enterprise* June 1993: 143-151.

Brown, Carolyn M. "United We Stand." *Black Enterprise* June 1997: 191-221.

Hall, Charles E. *Negroes in the United States, 1920-1932.* Washington, DC: Commerce Department, 1935.

Jones, Joyce. "Seeking a New Policy for Growth." *Black Enterprise* June 1999: 215-220.

Mack, Gracian. "B.E. Financials Overview." *Black Enterprise* June 1995: 157-161.

McCoy, Frank. "Life Sustaining Measures." *Black Enterprise* June 1998: 182-189.

Ofari, Earl. *The Myth of Black Capitalism.* New York: Monthly Review Press, 1970.

Schmidt, Jr., Charles, E. "Annuities Lead Growth in Net Premiums Written." *Best's Review: Life/Health Insurance Edition* July 1995: 14-17.

Scott, Matthew S., and Wendy C. Pelle. "B.E. Financial Overview." *Black Enterprise* June 1996:160-173.

Survey of Minority-owned Business Enterprise-Black. Washington, DC: Commerce Department, 2000.

Sweeney, Patrick, M. "Shifting to High Gear." *Best's Review: Life/Health Insurance Edition* July 1997: 26-31.

Van Deburg, William L. *New Day in Babylon: The Black Power Movement and American Culture, 1965-1985.* Chicago: U of Chicago P, 1992.

Walker, Juliet E.K. *The History of Black Business in America: Capitalism, Race, Entrepreneurship.* New York: Macmillan/Twayne, 1998.

Weems, Jr., Robert E., and Lewis A. Randolph. "The Ideological Origins of Richard M. Nixon's 'Black Capitalism' Initiative." *The Review of Black Political Economy.* 29 (2001): 49-61.

Weems, Jr., Robert, E. "Bling-Bling and other Recent Trends in African American Consumerism." *African Americans in the U.S. Economy.* Cecilia A. Conrad, John Whitehead, Patrick Mason, and James Stewart, eds. Lanham, MD: Rowman and Littlechild, 2005. 252-257.

——. "Black America During the 1960s: What Really Happened?" *Western Journal of Black Studies* 14 (1990): 153-158.

——. "A Blueprint for African American Economic Development." *Western Journal of Black Studies* 17 (1993): 96-100.

——. "A Crumbling Legacy: The Decline of African American Insurance Companies in Contemporary America." *The Review of Black Political Economy* 23 (1994): 25-37.

4

Three Concepts of Legitimacy

Winston A. Van Horne

This short essay is excerpted from the lectures of my course on *Urban Violence*, which I have given for over a quarter century. Throughout the years, my students, all too many of whom have been touched very directly by violence in the city, have found the presentation on legitimacy to be especially valuable in regard to their own everyday lives. Given the lively discussions that have usually accompanied my presentation on legitimacy, I have finally decided that it would be well to share with a non-classroom audience what I have been saying in the classroom. No dissertation on legitimacy is presented here. I simply offer the three concepts of legitimacy that I have used in my course based upon long years of study and reflection and the observations of the many hundreds of students who have found the concepts to be useful in coming to grips with the brutality of violence that ever so many of them have confronted in their daily lives.

There are three basic concepts of legitimacy: legal legitimacy, moral legitimacy, and social legitimacy. The positive law is the foundation of legal legitimacy; moral precepts ground moral legitimacy; social legitimacy emanates from the prevailing norms, mores, and ethos of a given community or society.

Legal legitimacy flows from the authority of the positive law, and entails conduct that is consistent with the prescriptions and proscriptions law, that is, lawful behavior. Legal legitimacy and legal authority are one and the same, and legitimacy is simply a synonym for lawfulness, having no independent conceptual or empirical content apart from legality. Legitimacy is thus tautologous with legality, and gives no new information to the world concerning lawfulness aside from already established procedural and substantive tenets of the positive law. And law, the positive law (1) consists of all the rules of conduct, principles, and regulations

47

established by the authority, legislation, or custom of a given community or society; (2) is applicable to all of those who are covered by the reach of its jurisdiction and authority; and (3) is enforced by judicial or administrative decisions and police powers. Legality legitimacy thus presumes conduct that conforms to the prescriptions and proscriptions of law.

Law, observes Thomas Hobbes, in general, is not Counsel but Command; nor a Command of any man to any man; but only of him, whose Command is addressed to one formerly obliged to obey him.[1] And the Civil Law, *Is to every Subject, those Rules, which the Common-wealth hath Commanded him, by Word, Writing, or other sufficient Sign of the Will, to make use of, for the Distinction of Right, and Wrong; that is to say, of what is contrary, and what is not contrary to the Rule.*[2] To Hobbes, and Hans Kelsen would agree, the positive law by command prescribes conduct that is right, and proscribes behavior that is wrong. Right and wrong here are not moral-ethical terms but legal ones. Indeed, Kelsen notes that the concept of law [as it is developed in his *General Theory of Law and State*] has no moral connotation whatsoever. It [merely] designates *a specific technique of social organization*. The problem of law, as a scientific problem, is the problem of social technique, not a problem of morals.[3] In relation to the positive law as a social technique, right simply means lawful and wrong unlawful, and legitimacy entails behavior that conforms to the prescriptions and proscriptions of law.

Without recognizing it explicitly, Frantz Fanon, a primary theoretician of the Algerian Revolution of the 1960s, for example, makes use of the concept of legal legitimacy when he observes that [t]he colonial regime owes its legitimacy to force,[4] through which the native is coerced to obey. By controlling the state, and through it the form and substance of the positive law, the colonial regime is able to overspread the force that it uses against the native with the color of law. Force is thus made legal and, tautologously, legitimate. This is not, of course, the case with all regimes. The legal legitimacy of force may well be complemented by moral legitimacy, which elicits obedience voluntarily.

Moral legitimacy is a virtue, and embraces rectitude, decency, integrity, fidelity, trustworthiness, and natural compassion. Just as wherever legal legitimacy obtains, legal authority also obtains. In like manner moral legitimacy is coextensive with moral authority. By its authority, moral legitimacy draws limits concerning permissible and impermissible conduct. Those limits may be broader, or narrower, or the same as the ones set by legal legitimacy, contingent on the logic of the situation at hand. The moral authority of legitimacy does not always recognize boundaries drawn by legal authority, and breeches them whenever and wherever its integrity is violated. This point is of the utmost importance, for it signals clearly and distinctly that imperatives emanating from the moral authority of legitimacy may not always be consonant with commands issuing from the legal authority of law. Moreover, it affords grounds for questioning, disputing, opposing, protesting, and even fighting with arms prescriptions and proscriptions of the positive law.

If problems of the positive law are ones of social technique, which are separate and distinct from ones of morals, as Kelsen believes, substantial asymmetries often obtain between the imperatives of moral legitimacy and the demands of legal legitimacy. A given positive law, or a given act under the color of a particular positive law, may well be considered to be lawful and right by some, but nonetheless be perceived as illegitimate and wrong by others.

Consider, for example, the following passage from Martin Luther King's Letter from Birmingham City Jail. Writing to his fellow clergymen in defense of his intentional and deliberate violation of laws prescribing racial segregation, King says:

> You express a great deal of anxiety over our willingness to break laws [that is, to act illegally]. This is certainly a legitimate concern. . . . One may well ask, How can you advocate breaking some laws and obeying others? The answer is found in the fact that there are two types of laws: There are *just* and there are *unjust* laws. I would agree with Saint Augustine that An unjust law is no law at all.
>
> Now what is the difference between the two? How does one determine when a law is just or unjust? A just law is a man-made code that squares with the moral law or the law of God. An unjust law is a code that is out of harmony with the moral law. To put it in the terms of Saint Thomas Aquinas [here King taps Aquinas' fourfold division of law], an unjust law is a human law that is not rooted in eternal and natural law. Any law that uplifts human personality is just. Any law that degrades human personality is unjust. All segregation statutes are unjust because segregation distorts the soul and damages the personality. It gives the segregator a false sense of superiority, and the segregated a false sense of inferiority.[5]

It is King's belief that all segregation statutes are odious, unjust, wrong, and morally offensive, that is, illegitimate, even though they may have been approved legally under the techniques of the positive law, having satisfied all of the relevant procedures for the enactment of their substance. But being out of tune with eternal law and natural law, segregation statutes, though legal, are morally illegitimate, and so do not command his allegiance. It is not right, fitting, or proper, he believes, that one should willingly obey statutes which distort one's soul, and degrade as well as damage one's personality. King is well aware that he has a legal duty to obey the segregation statutes against which he protests, but he also believes strongly that he has no moral duty to do so. And for him, moral duty takes precedence over legal duty, any command of the positive law to the contrary notwithstanding. Thus he disobeys the law, and pays the societal cost of his disobedience. The imperative of moral legitimacy here is disobedience; the command of legal legitimacy is obedience.

King's conflation of law and justice puts him squarely at odds with Kelsen, who makes plain that [t]here are legal orders which are, from a certain point of view, unjust. [But l]aw and justice are two different concepts. Law as distinguished from justice is positive law. [6] King abides no such distinction between law and justice. (The concepts of law posited by King and Kelsen call out starkly a perennial problem in political philosophy and jurisprudence, namely, the proper relation between law and justice.) By conflating law and justice, he constructs grounds on which one may stand to legitimately disobey what one perceives to be unjust laws. As an ardent believer in the principle of nonviolence, King makes plain that [o]ne who breaks an unjust law must do it *openly, lovingly* . . . and with a willingness to accept the penalty. [And] submit[s] that an individual who breaks a law that conscience tells him is unjust, and willingly accepts the penalty by staying in jail to arouse the conscience of the community over its injustice, *is in reality expressing the very highest respect for law.* [7]

But why should, say, a native ever express the highest respect for the law of the settler; or a colonized person the law of the colonial overlord; or the victim of a pogrom the law of the pogromist; or the occupied of the occupier; or any oppressed individual the law of the ones who oppress him/her? Such respect either is purely expediential in the context of an extant correlation of forces, or a manifestation of what I call the neurosis of oppression, that is, an inner compulsion to obey where obedience should not be given.

Fanon, for example, does not abide nonviolence as a principle of social action for the liberation of the oppressed, and could not countenance anyone who is oppressed willingly evincing the highest respect for laws that presume his inferiority and constrain severely his life chances. It has been noted already that he believes colonial regimes owe their legitimacy to force and, as such, have no moral authority to command the allegiance of the colonized. Accordingly, absent force buttressed by legal authority, the settler has no authority over the native, hence the native need not obey as long as he can get away with his disobedience. For force never can be the foundation of the moral authority of legitimacy, thus colonial regimes that owe their legitimacy to force have no moral legitimacy in relation to those who suffer their rule. Being legal within the framework of the laws of the colonizer but morally illegitimate in the context of the culture and society of the colonized, colonial/settler regimes, generally lacking the authority of moral legitimacy, are continually at risk of subversion by the native.

Colonial regimes have been a historical reality, but they also stand as a metaphor and symbol for force and power devoid of the moral authority of legitimacy. Where legality obtains without moral legitimacy, individuals may well dispose themselves of a variety of means, including acts of violence, to alter the conditions of legality that prevail. Contrariwise, where legal legitimacy is reinforced by moral legitimacy and legal authority undergirded by moral authority, the sort of oppression called out by Fanon in *The Wretched of the Earth*, and the chronic condition of civil war mentioned by St. Augustine in *The City of God*, generally do not obtain. For whereas legal legitimacy is often impelled to command obedience through coercion, moral legitimacy always elicits obedience without coercion. And coercion is the fang and poison of oppression. Moral legitimacy thus defangs oppression under the color of law. Aiming always and without exception to foster that which is right, fitting, and proper in relation to norms of human decency and sound principles of natural compassion, moral legitimacy seeks to improve the human condition and preserve the supreme law of civilization, that is, the full nurture, growth, and development of humankind.

Accordingly, an act is morally legitimate if it: (1) sustains or restores norms of human decency; (2) adds credit to one's store of trustworthiness and integrity; (3) inhibits, if not prevents, the worsening of a state of affairs that affects the freedom and well-being of individuals and/or groups; (4) occasions some betterment of a particular societal state; (5) is deemed to be right, fitting, and proper by disinterested others; and (6) is consistent with behaviors and practices that are worthy of emulation in regard to civilized conduct. Moral legitimacy overspreads an act with a spirit of rectitude, giving it a standing in propriety and probity that it otherwise would not have. There is much attractiveness here, but there is something awfully important that has yet to be brought into focus, that is, the concept of social legitimacy.

Social legitimacy entails the shared norms, beliefs, and attitudes of a tribe, clan, racial/ethnic grouping, community, nation, state, or society concerning the utility, value, desirability, acceptability, and appropriateness of given behaviors and their outcomes. It is thus highly variable, as is also true of legal legitimacy. Just as the positive law varies from community to community, nation to nation, and state to state, so, too, will that which is deemed to be socially legitimate. The variability of social legitimacy tends to foster domains of competing, as well as conflicting, legitimacies. Here different, sometimes radically different, conceptions and perceptions of utility, value, desirability, acceptability, and appropriateness collide as individuals and groups press their respective claims. Consider the lynching of black people in the United States, for example.

For roughly three generations–from the 1880s through the 1940s–especially in the states of the ex-Confederacy–the lynching of blacks was commonplace in the United States.[8] Lynching was commonly a community affair. White lawyers, teachers, doctors, coroners, clergymen, businessmen, as well as so-called ordinary folk, including children, would wallow in the vile orgy and vulgar festivity suffused with the frenzy of excitement that invariably attended the obscene spectacle of a lynching. Reporting the burning at the stake of twenty-year-old Richard Coleman of Maysville, Kentucky, at noon on December 6, 1899, for the assault and murder of a young white woman, the *New York World* of December 7, 1899, noted that Coleman was lynched *in the presence of thousands of [white] men, and hundreds of [white] women and children.* It continued:

> Tortures almost unbelievable were inflicted upon the wretched negro. In all the vast crowd that witnessed the agonies of the man, *not one hand was raised in humanity's behalf, nor a single voice heard in the interest of mercy.* Instead, when some new torture was inflicted upon the shrieking, burning boy, the crowd cheered and cheered, the shrill voices of women and the piping tones of children sounding high above the roar of men.
>
> Not one person in the crowd wore a mask. The leaders of the mob disdained the semblance of any disguise. *Every act was done in the open. There was no secrecy.* The population of the whole city and country for miles around, church men and church women, professional and business men of eminence, people of distinguished ancestry, formed the mob, and not a single regret for the horrible tragedy [could] be heard . . . from one end of the town to the other. . . .
>
> Long after most of the mob went away little children from six to ten years of age carried dried grass and kindling wood and kept the fire burning all during the afternoon.
>
> Relic-hunters visited the scene and carried away pieces of flesh and the negro's teeth. Others got pieces of fingers and toes and proudly exhibit[ed] the ghastly souvenirs. . . .
>
> The Coroner held an inquest [that] evening, and rendered a verdict that *Coleman came by his death at the hands of unknown persons.*[9]

And so went lynchings in all too many a community: [D]eath at the hands of parties unknown was the usual verdict for black men accused with the usual crime, that is, the actual or putative assault and/or murder of a white woman.[10]

In an intriguing discussion of lynching in *Rituals of Blood*, Orlando Patterson observes that the lynchings of blacks were notably sacrificial and highly ritualistic. They were also full of drama and play culminating in the sacrifice of the victim. Because the sacrifices did not take place in already consecrated places such as churches, the use of fire as a consecrating agent became necessary, in this way serving the multiple functions of consecration, torture, and the divine devouring of the victim's soul. The stakes to which the victims were tied were obviously consecrated in the process also, since they [as well as charred remains of the victim's body] became relics to be treasured.[11] Sacrifice and ritual were socially legitimizing attributes of lynching. They transformed sheer wickedness into conduct that was deemed to be desirable, appropriate, acceptable, valuable, and useful for the lynchers and their community. Indeed, Patterson opines that one element of the utility of ritual lynchings lay in affording a literal measure of cannibalistic satisfaction to the appetites of the lynchers through the olfactory taste of burning black flesh. He writes:

> The common observation that our sense of taste is strongly related to our sense of smell, and that tasting is in large part actually smelling, has now been scientifically proven. In particular, the psychophysicist Claire Murphy has demonstrated that a near perfect additivity exists between odorants and tastants and that there is no true sensory inhibition between olfaction and taste. In layman's language, this means that taste and smell stimulants add up to the same sensation and that their effects are not perceived differently by the brain. The experience, then, of being suffused with the odor of the lynch victim's roasting body amounted literally to the cannibalistic devouring of his body. . . .
>
> Southern lynchers did not have to await the modern scientific study of olfaction to realize that they were actually eating the Afro-American sacrificial victim as they consumed the fumes from his burning body and went around savoring little pieces of his barbecued flesh. This scientific finding has long been anticipated by the Bible. Every fundamentalist Southerner, thoroughly versed in the Old Testament language of sacrifice, would be aware of the classic biblical descriptions . . . of how God consumed the sacrificial burnt offering–by smelling the soothing odor and consuming the sweet savor of the animal's burning flesh. . . .
>
> [Additionally,] the cooked Negro, properly roasted, [had] been tamed and culturally transformed and [could] now be eaten, communally, in imitation of the Euro-Americans' own God savoring his burnt offering.[12]

My purpose in citing Patterson at length is not to raise contestation about the soundness of his proffer concerning the literal cannibalism of lynchings in the United States. It is, rather, to call out that a legally heinous (illegitimate) and morally vile (illegitimate) act may nonetheless be socially desirable, acceptable, appropriate, valuable, and useful (legitimate) for the ones who participate in it. Social legitimacy oftentimes confounds legal illegitimacy and moral illegitimacy as its beneficiaries refuse to concede any illegality or immorality in their conduct. This occasions substantial strains, tensions, vexations, and conflicts in a political society as claimants of legal legitimacy and moral legitimacy press hard to alter what they perceive to be socially illegitimate behavior(s). (Incidentally, the legal illegitimacy of the burning of Coleman was recognized by a Judge Wadsworth, a participant in the orgy, who said: I am a police judge, but for once perhaps *I forgot the duties of the office*. [James] Lashbrook [the husband of the deceased woman] has my sympathy. [13]) By the 1940s, the hard work of anti-lynching advocates in the United States had paid off markedly in a substantial decrease in lynchings across the United States, even though Congress never passed an anti-lynching law. The asymmetry of lynching being socially legitimate in given communities but legally illegitimate as well as morally illegitimate in most of the land dissolved as a symmetry between social illegitimacy, legal illegitimacy, and moral illegitimacy increasingly overspread the society *vis-à-vis* lynching.

The extent to which the social, legal, and moral illegitimation of lynching had become embedded in American society by the end of the twentieth century was evident in the local and national response to the lynching of James Byrd, Jr., a black man, in Jasper, Texas. Byrd, a former vacuum cleaner salesman, was abducted [by three young white males] early on June 7, 1998, and taken to a remote area northeast of Jasper. His ankles were harnessed with a 24[.5]-foot logging chain to the bumper of a pickup truck and he was dragged for three miles. His battered torso, minus his head, neck and an arm, was dumped between a black church and cemetery where it was found a few hours after daylight. The circumstances of the crime provoked a national outrage, [14] as well as much grief and sorrow in Jasper. Two of Byrd's lynchers were sentenced to death, and the third to life imprisonment. How strikingly does the *social illegitimacy* of the lynching of James Byrd in Jasper at the end of the twentieth century contrast with the *social legitimacy* of the lynching of Richard Coleman in Maysville at the end of the nineteenth century?

One does not wish to make an empirical generalization from a single illustration, but I dare say that at the outset of twenty-first-century America there is a greater correspondence between social legitimacy, legal legitimacy, and moral legitimacy in relation to the cohesion of the political society than there was at the outset of twentieth-century America—the many frictions, quarrels, vexations, and distresses that abound notwithstanding. This affords grounds for optimism concerning at least the near-term future of American society, for wherever social, legal, and moral legitimacy conflate strongly are the societal strands that they weave together. One, though, should ever be mindful of the societal costs that invariably attend admixtures of social, legal, and moral legitimacy and illegitimacy, especially where sharp asymmetries obtain.

Notes

1. Thomas Hobbes, *Leviathan*, C.B. MacPherson, ed. (New York: Penguin Books, 1984), Part II, Ch. XXVI.
2. Ibid.
3. Hans Kelsen, *General Theory of Law and State* (Cambridge, MA.: Harvard University Press, 1945), p. 5. Author's italics.
4. Franz Fanon, *The Wretched of the Earth,* trans. Constance Farrington (New York: Grove Press, Inc., 1968), p. 84.
5. Martin Luther King, Jr., Letter from Birmingham City Jail in *Civil Disobedience: Theory and Practice*, Hugo Adam Bedau, ed. (New York: Pegasus, 1969), p. 77.
6. Kelsen, op. cit. note 3, p. 5.
7. King, op. cit. note 5, pp. 78-79. Author's italics.
8. The book *100 Years of Lynching*, Ralph Ginzburg, ed. (Baltimore, MD: Black Classic Press, c1968) gives a A Partial Listing of Approximately 5,000 [Blacks] Lynched in [the] United States Since 1859, pp. 253-270.
9. 9. Roasted Alive, *New York World*, December 7, 1899, reprinted in *100 Years of Lynching*, pp. 24-30. Author's italics.
10. Ibid., pp. 17, 21.
11. Orlando Patterson, *Rituals of Blood: Consequences of Slavery in Two American Centuries* (Washington, DC: Civitas, 1998), p. 196.
12. Ibid., pp. 198-200. On the matter of the literal cannibalism of lynching, see pp. 197-202.
13. Ginzburg, op. cit. note 8, p. 29. Author's italics.
14. *MSNBC News*, Brewer get[s] death penalty for murder, http://www.msnbc.com/msn/314973.asp, 9/23/1999, p. 2.

5

The Culture Nexus Construct in Africana Studies

Cecil A. Blake

Africana Studies or its variants represent a cluster of "studies" such as Women's Studies that have developed on interdisciplinary bases. Hence Africana Studies, Pan-African Studies, or Black Studies invariably offer courses in history, literature, and political science to name a few. The purpose of this article is to present a discussion on a construct advanced here—the culture nexus construct—as one means of investigating the status of Africana Studies and its *raison d'être*. The underlying assumption that informs the construct is that any discipline or "studies" that is interdisciplinary-based periodically undergoes diagnosis with subsequent interventions proffered. The culture nexus construct is advanced in this work as a diagnostic tool used to investigate the intellectual environment within which Africana Studies functions. The construct provides a handle as to how to discover, in the first instance, elements within the intellectual environment that represent exigencies, and secondly proffer interventions which may be most conducive in resolving the exigencies with implications for Africana Studies.

In this paper, I provide a definition through analogies of what constitutes the culture nexus and discuss its potential for assisting in fashioning interventions in singular or systemic dimensions by use of an application of the construct in the subject areas of jurisprudence, rhetoric, and literature, concluding with implications for Africana Studies.

The Culture Nexus Construct

In setting the stage for this presentation it is incumbent upon me to provide a definition of the construct and through the exercise, a rationale. I venture to do so by taking the liberty of making an excursion into medicine as my point of departure. When we contract any form of respiratory ailment and visit the doctor, he/she asks us to open our mouths and then proceeds to place the swab just at the entrance of our throats. We are then asked to cough, in order to collect specimen that is processed resulting in a culture, an essential step in the diagnostic procedure. The results from tests applied in the culture determine the type—singular or broad spectrum—of interventions required to cure the ailment; in other words, resolve the exigency.

The importance of using the medical analogies above, to my mind, is fundamental: (a) without testing and analyzing the culture as described above, the doctor may not get a full understanding of the type of ailment, and the diagnosis may not be complete or accurate; (b) with the culture obtained and diagnosis arrived at, specific interventions in the forms of medication/treatment sharply targeting the type of infection can be identified and applied; (c) as patterns of diagnosis and therapy progress, coupled with vigorous research and development, broad spectrum treatment may be discovered—as in broad spectrum antibiotics, that cover more than one type of infection. The culture nexus construct advanced in this work is predicated on the diagnostic procedure above, applied within societal contexts—in this instance, applied within the context of the disciplines identified earlier.

We must bear in mind, however, that the complexities involved with diagnosing cultures may, on the one hand, reveal mutations that make it difficult to come up with interventions necessary to "cure" the ailment. On the other hand, such mutations may have a "positive" effect particularly if we make extrapolations of such mutations in cultures found in human societies.

A clear example of what may be considered one of such results is the disruption of cultures in societies that were invaded, dominated, and/or colonized. European colonialism and Arab invasions in parts of Africa resulted in the formation of a "language" that is morphologically neither indigenous nor European or Arab. "Creolized" languages evolved that mimic the colonizers language as well as those of the colonized societies. The "Krio" language in Sierra Leone and Kiswahili in East Africa are examples. They represent a medium that is more widely used across ethnic boundaries than the invading language or languages directly linked to specific ethnic groups. The use of the term "positive" in this example refers to the possibility for interethnic communication by use of the creolized language among different ethnic groups, hence facilitating communicative interactions.

What follows, is an application of the construct in terms of both its diagnostic component and the fashioning of intervention strategies, using as examples, jurisprudence, rhetoric and literature, concluding with the implications for Africana Studies. Let me adumbrate.

The Culture Nexus and Jurisprudence

We have legal systems in African states such as Sierra Leone that create confusion for many. Let us use an imaginary swab and extract a specimen, cultivate a culture and test it, in search of the legal elements (regimes) upon which jurisprudence is predicated in Sierra Leone, for example, and many former British colonies for that matter. The culture obtained represents elements that are African and European, consistent with the colonial legacy. In Sierra Leone, there are two legal systems—one inherited from the colonial past, laws made by Parliament; and Sierra Leone/African customary law, practiced in geographical areas, usually rural, with a preponderance of a given ethnic group. Legal regimes manifest cultural roots on which warrants and the idea of justice are found, grounded in the history and traditions of their sources of origin, and influenced as well by the environment.

A simple example of how such cultural dimensions and environmental conditions are manifest in the "Laws of Sierra Leone," based in part on the British legal tradition, could substantiate my claim. Lawyers and judges in Sierra Leone cannot participate in court proceedings without wearing blond-haired (as in Caucasian) wigs, warranted on Eurocentric legal traditions. In addition to the wigs, the temperature may be in the nineties, or even warmer, yet practitioners are required to satisfy dress codes—full western suits—that are terribly inconvenient for the climate in Sierra Leone during the dry season.

Thus even in appearance, some may wonder as to why these Africans dress the way they do to go to court, sweating and seething in heat just to conform to alien warrants and codes. From this perspective, diagnostically, we have a situation in which legal regimes that constitute the "laws of Sierra Leone" are culled in part from the colonial past and serve as basis for adjudication and redress. Of interest in the diagnostic exercise utilizing the culture nexus construct is the extent to which customary laws could be applied nationally, as contrasted to its invocation only as it may apply to geographic locations based on ethnicity, as a means of redressing conflicts and legal breaches in a less cumbersome and cost effective manner.

Yet another outcome of the diagnosis in contemporary Sierra Leone reveal another malaise requiring some form of intervention. The deliberations of the Special Court of Sierra Leone set up by the United Nations and the Government of Sierra Leone to try those responsible for the gravest breaches of international humanitarian laws during the ten-year gruesome conflict in the country (1991-2001) represent a type of crisis involved in fashioning interventions to deal with the malaise diagnosed. The legal regimes in use in the Special Court are international humanitarian laws and the laws of Sierra Leone. Even though customary laws represent a constituent element within the laws of Sierra Leone, they are not being invoked even in circumstances where the crimes committed are in areas with a preponderance of given ethnic groups. The argument here is not that customary laws should singularly be isolated and used as the basis for adjudication, but rather that certain aspects of the "spirit" of customary laws may serve purposes in addition to punitive outcome of the adjudication process. The implication for the preceding claim with regard to the Special Court mainly involves a possible dimension of reconciliation and social cohesion following a gruesome war perpetrated by youths and their leaders from geographic regions with a preponderance of given ethnic groups respectively.

Stemming from the above, the legal instruments in use during the trial have punitive measures that may serve justice at the end, but derail reconciliation and social cohesion with a resultant society that may suffer a relapse of the gruesome war. This is said against the background of possible guilty judgments that would be rendered against the leader of the Civil Defense Forces Sam Hinga Norman, who defended the country against the rebels, and a key figure among the rebel leadership "General" Issa Seasy, who successfully persuaded the rebels to disarm and respect the accords of the Lome Peace Accords that brought the war to an end. There is a significant cross section of the country that regards the prosecution of the two as being unjustified. The basis for the discontent may be understood and perhaps influenced by attitudes informed by customary laws towards punishment and reconciliation that ensure, at the end, social cohesion.

Fashioning intervention strategies for the diagnosis above would involve raising questions about what would constitute ingredients of the chosen intervention(s): specific or broad spectrum. Given the complexity of the diagnosis, one may rule out without much argument the possibility of a broad intervention. Among the possible questions that may be asked are the following: how do we deal with the issues of justice being served, punishment meted out, but reconciliation and social cohesion possibly thwarted as a result of an inherent conflict with societal attitude towards reconciliation, social cohesion and healing grounded in customary laws?

The gravity of the crimes committed call for banishment from given ethnic communities in which customary laws apply. Yet, there is a cultural orientation which appears to have a national character that dissuades extreme actions such as banishment. For instance, there are many activities associated with the forest in Sierra Leonean folklore. Secret societies such as the "*poro*" (for males) perform a lot of their socialization processes for the youths, such as hunting, and so on, in the forest. Reference to the forest is therefore common. There is a common expression, for example, which states: "A 'bad' bush (or forest) does not exist where 'bad' children should be sent into exile because of crimes committed by them." This expression is fundamentally not consistent with the idea of "banishment" mentioned above.

Thus even in customary laws that have punitive measures which include banishment from a given community, there appears to be a contradiction, given the cultural orientation mentioned above. Perhaps a clearly defined Africana theory or theories culled from cultural belief systems and orientations regarding the incorporation and invocation of customary legal regimes within a national rather than a parochial context, may help in fashioning the type of specific intervention required to treat the perceived malaise diagnosed.

The task is to engage in research and other forms of exploration (as we shall see later during the discussion on the culture nexus construct and rhetoric), that would yield Africana based theories as far as African jurisprudence is concerned, which may shed some light on how to go about fashioning methodologies for interventions necessary to treat the malaise. As Joko Smart states, "Sierra Leone Law has generated far less attention than a discipline of its importance demands. Hitherto, particular focus has been directed by lawyers at the General Law which is basically English Law, whilst the Indigenous Law has been overwhelmingly ignored even though the vast majority of the peoples of the country are governed by Customary Law in their family relationships" (1983, p. v.).

Essentially, therefore, the culture nexus construct provides a handle for diagnosing the nature of the composite legal environment of Sierra Leone. Furthermore, it assists in determining the nature of the intervention(s) required for the resolution of observed exigencies. The interventions arrived at may have possible interfaces with those found in customary laws, international humanitarian laws as well as the laws of Sierra Leone, culminating in institutionalizing legal regimes that may reflect recognition and application of punitive actions, but carried out within the context of attitudes toward reconciliation, social cohesion, and societal healing consistent with customary legal regimes. If this is achieved, it would exemplify how the culture nexus works within the context of African jurisprudence. Let us now move on to rhetoric.

The Culture Nexus and Rhetoric

If one were to extract a culture from the corpus of theories, concepts, methods, and so on, in the field of rhetoric and perform a diagnosis of it, the following would be readily discernible. It would reveal that, traditionally, the study of rhetoric was concerned with examining theories and methods that guide the generation, organization, style and delivery of persuasive messages addressed to large audiences in a discursive manner. Its concern was public address, with a speaker addressing an audience. Such utterances produce, according to Golden et al. "timeless and historically significant public address performances as Socrates's 'Apology,' Edmund Burke's election speech in 1780, and Lincoln's Gettysburg address. In each of these instances," they continue, "the ideas being articulated spoke not only to the immediate audiences but to people in subsequent ages. In short, discourse at its best emphasizes values that are to be learned anew by each generation" (1992, p. xi). Furthermore, we will see that rhetoric as a subject and speech act/performance is inherently culture bound, and that rhetorical criticism cannot be successfully done without locating the text within its cultural setting. Campbell and Burkholder state, "to interpret a rhetorical act, critics need information about the context in which the act occurred ... context also includes the cultural milieu and the climate of opinion in which the rhetorical act appears" (1997, p. 51). We see clearly from above the powerful imagery of the culture as nexus, since rhetorical acts are deeply enmeshed in culture.

As a discipline, rhetorical communication studies provide research and training, the results of which prepares the speaker to communicate with audiences with the hope of getting them to become convinced about a proposition, as in the forensic genre, or take action so as to benefit from the speakers propositions, as in the deliberative genre. Essentially, the major rhetorical genres are forensic (messages of lawyers addressed to judges and jury in the law courts) or deliberative (messages addressed to audiences involved in deliberations in political entities such as Parliament, congress, or even in corporate or non-corporate settings where the objective is to come up with policies that would be beneficial for all). These two genres utilize arguments as strategies for developing their messages. The arguments are structured around Western modes of proof—logos, ethos, and pathos—with artistic and non-artistic proofs to energize evidence used in support of a claim/proposition. The third genre—epidiectic—in the Aristotelian classification was presumably non-argumentative and restricted in a way to the celebration of values worthy of perpetuation and necessary for the promotion of social cohesion (Blake, 1995).

Each genre, therefore, comes with its distinct goal, tools, and procedures that ensure the development, organization, and delivery of messages through the speech act. The rhetorical theorist conducts research and teaches theory. The rhetorical critic analyzes the discourse, using as frames of reference theories, tools, strategies, and so on, germane to the genre of the given discourse and illuminates how successfully the message was generated, organized, and delivered and with what effect or impact. The responsibility of those trained in rhetorical theory and criticism, therefore, is to study and impart knowledge about theories and methods that inform and guide rhetorical communication.

In 1970, however, a major diagnosis of the state of the art of rhetorical studies was done at Wingspread in Racine, Wisconsin. I regard this diagnosis as an equivalent to the diagnosis procedure utilized in the culture nexus construct advanced in this paper. Upon completion of the diagnosis, a broad spectrum intervention was identified and applied, and the result was the emergence of the "new rhetoric," which expanded the realm of rhetoric not just to the messages of speakers in public address contexts, but to writers (both literary and dramatic), poets, and agitators and their use of both discursive and non-discursive communication strategies in social movements and revolutions. The new rhetoric also gave validity to the claims of Perelman that pre-dated Wingspread, who had argued earlier that the epidiectic genre does have a persuasive element since speeches in the genre predispose audiences, potentially, to be persuaded in future rhetorical contexts.

Central to this development after Wingspread is an added dimension and importance of looking at messages and how they are developed and relayed. The messages in essence become "stories" and "acts" in some instances as they seek to communicate intentions. The speaker or writer or actor becomes a story-teller of events—historical and contemporary—highlighting themes on culture, values, ideologies, conflicts, alienation, and so on, as he or she crafts and/or conveys the message to his or her intended and even unintended audiences. Thus, how the story is told, the tools used to construct it, and the style in which it is delivered becomes part and parcel of the province of rhetoric.

Even though Kenneth Burke had provided us with the pentad, coupled with his theory of identification and consubstantiality, Wingspread formalized the expanded conceptualization of rhetorical theory and criticism. Instead of relying heavily on the tools of rationalistic criticism—videlicet invention, arrangement, style, delivery, and memory—we observe the formal introduction of psychosocial criticism, that focus on audience adaptation and pathos, psychosocial structure of sequential argumentative strategy, and a linking of rational and psychosocial factors as critics sought to illuminate their analysis the best way possible. Burke's *Dramatistic Pentad* gave rise to dramatistic criticism, with focus on language and symbols informed as well by his theory of identification and consubstantiality mentioned above (1968, 1969).

The aftermath of Wingspread further strengthened the bases for an understanding of the inextricable linkage between rhetorical communication and literature. Wingspread, as a conscious act by scholars keen to see how rhetoric should be understood against the background of prevailing exigencies, decided to extract a culture from the nexus, which was subsequently diagnosed with a broad spectrum intervention applied in the form of the "new rhetoric."

What Wingspread did as a diagnostic tool for testing the "culture" extracted from rhetorical communication studies in the west, Africana Studies as a discipline can do for rhetorical communication studies in Africa and its diaspora. When Africana Studies do emerge as a discipline, it would have a set of questions that it asks that are quite different from those asked by rhetoric as a discipline. It is precisely in this regard that I argue here that Africana Studies represent the best agency through which the culture nexus construct can be applied in our search for consistent constituent elements that would characterize theories of Africana rhetoric. There are a handful of publications—among them my work on traditional African values and the right to communicate (Blake, 1993 and Ugboajah, 1989)—which represent specific, as contrasted with systemic, interventions as we work towards an understanding and unearthing of an African system of rhetoric and communication.

In the Africana context, a lot of work has been done in African-American rhetoric, but not on Caribbean, South American and other diaspora communities' rhetoric. Diagnostic "tests" performed by African-American scholars on public address theory, for instance, revealed a peculiar malaise. Whereas public address theory within a Eurocentric context explains the act as one person speaking to many uninterrupted, African-American public address encourages an engagement in the form of exchanges (known as call-response) between the speaker and his/audience as the public address is delivered. Let us move on to African literature.

The Culture Nexus and African Literature

African literature continues to manifest a rigorous dialogue about its being, praxis, and analysis. As a subject, scholars have extracted a culture in the sense used throughout this paper and are engaged in a diagnostic exercise. Mudimbe for instance posits, "When we speak of African literature we refer to both a body of texts whose authors are known and to anonymous discourses which carry successive deposits of supposedly unknown imaginations" (1989, p.7). He also asks, "Could we arrive at any explicative norms which will put it in some sort of relation with other literatures and not give us the uncomfortable feeling that it is somehow an indigenized imitation of something else, or an adapted reproduction of psychological confusions imported from the West?" (p. 7). What Mudimbe clearly demonstrates is the fact that African literature is definitely steps ahead of rhetorical communication in terms of diagnostic exercises and piecemeal interventions. African literature scholars are busy in so many ways asking questions and advancing concepts and theories in trying to diagnose and discover, preferably, systemic interventions clearly with the culture nexus as construct. As with rhetoric, African literature is culture bound, with added complexities of regional, ethnic, linguistic, and colonial legacies at play.

It is interesting to note that Mudimbe also argues that "African literature as a commodity is a recent phenomenon and authors as well as critics tend to resist this fact" (p. 7). There is, of course, recognition of *orature,* Africa's oral tradition, and its influence on African literature even though ramifications for factors—like audience reach and adaptation, stylistic devices and the interactive dimension: audience/performer relationship—represent serious theoretical and methodological implications. Making a linkage between *orature* and African literature, however, would suggest Africa's ancient and continued penchant for story-telling orally, an act that the African literary writer does through the print medium.

In addressing the topic of the idea of African literature being a recent phenomenon as it pertains to English language fiction from West Africa, Peters argues, however, that "While [African literature] has been in existence for perhaps too short a time for one to talk about a fully established tradition, a number of important phases, landmarks, themes, and trends distinguish its development ..." (p.9). He identifies three waves or phases, namely the first wave that brought to the fore, works by Tutuola, Ekwenzi, Achebe, Conton, Prince Modupeh and Onuora Nzekwu. The second wave he contends had "holdovers" with the emergence of Wole Soyinka, Ayi Kwei Armah, Gabriel Okara, Abioseh Nicol, Yulissa Maddy, and Sarif Easmon among others. The third wave also had "holdovers" with the emergence of Buchi Emeta, Obi Egbuna, Flora Nwapa, Adaora Lilly Ulasi and many others. All of these writers and their counterparts in the other regions of Africa address various themes. Peters identifies themes African literary writers highlight in their works such as corruption, graft, materialism, violence, alienation, culture, traditions, history, and so on. Essentially, African literature as agency engaged readers on issues of transition and problems arising from the process, embedded in realms that range from ideology to nostalgic renditions about the African past with apparent appeals by some to rediscover the pre-colonial African past.

Like rhetorical theory, African literature, as the themes above confirm, is deeply rooted in culture. African literature brings to our attention exigencies explained in an imaginative/fictional or non-fictional manner through the medium of writing. Since both disciplines deal with the human condition and seek through their various themes to articulate and/or celebrate values germane for social cohesion while pointing out as well negative machinations in society; the challenge in the diagnostic phase underway is how to arrive at an Africana theory as an intervention, on the basis of what is extant, following the colonial intrusion and the resultant society, and that which was "African" as in pre-colonial Africa.

It is this complex of identifying and diagnosing extant culture that gave rise to the scathing attack by Chudi Amuta (1989) against the well-known works of Chinweizu, et. al. (1980) and Wole Soyinka (1976). In order to engage in meaningful literary or rhetorical criticism, it is important to have a theoretical framework, even if eclectic, but preferably Africana. Amuta claims that there is a crisis in African literary criticism and explains the crisis thus: "The roots of the present crisis and disillusionment are not difficult to locate. The criticism of African literature as we have come to know it has been bedeviled by such ailments as (a) a false idealist, static, and undialectical conception of African society, (b) a faulty notion of the essence and nature of literature, (c) a near absence of clear theoretical moorings and (d) a preponderance of subjective (often intuitive) exegeses of isolated texts" (p.2). The issue here, to my mind, is not necessarily the veracity of his claims, but rather the projection of an image of something of a "discipline"—African literature—that has emerged presumably without adequate diagnosis, and subsequently, the provision of an intervention reflective of culture from which it is nurtured. Hence, he claims that the in the "bulk of discourse on African literature and culture, Africa is still conceived of as an undifferentiated socio-cultural continuum which has remained more or less oblivious to the passage of time" (p.2). He laments as well what he sees as a "disturbing theoretical anemia," pointing out theories from Europe such as "Freudian psychoanalysis, phenomenology, structuralism, new criticism, [and] formalism," of which "our cultural intelligentsia have endlessly appropriated" applying them "often indiscriminately to aspects of African literature" (Ibid.).

Chinweizu, Jemie, Madubuike, and Soyinka, even though they are recognized by Amuta as providing works that provoke this form of discourse, were at the receiving end of his wrath. He is vexed by the bifurcation of what could be seen as an all out celebration, and albeit an apotheosis of a nostalgic African past, along the lines of Chiweizu's decolonization of African literature, and what he considers Soyinka's thrust on the West. Ironically, however, he proffers a dialectical Marxist construct as the answer. Marxist dialectics would help, he contends, to explain the imperialist factor in terms of Africa's history and the impact on its culture. But at the end of the day, isn't Amuta himself locked into Eurocentric theoretical formulations that may not have the capacity to serve as an intervention worthy enough to address the Africana theoretical problematic? Isn't there room for an intervention that would enhance Africana theoretical and methodological formulations grounded in Africana thought?

The preceding discussion represent the issues that beg for attention against the background of applying culture nexus construct, as the community of scholars and diagnosticians engage the imperatives of the Africana Studies problematic, in search of interventions. The culture nexus construct provides us with a tool that facilitates diagnosis and the search for interventions that would bring to fruition knowledge necessary for an understanding of the epistemological, theoretical, methodological, professional, and pedagogical bases for Africana Studies as a discipline.

Unlike the Marxist theory and analysis that locates dialectical analysis primarily within economic relations and the centrality of understanding conflict as a tool for analysis, the culture nexus construct does not adopt, a priori, a given ideology as an entry point for the diagnostic exercise. It attempts, through induction, to study the "culture" extracted and come up with relevant interventions. I consider the exchanges among African literature scholars to represent the diagnostic phase. Even though there is no time frame allotted for such a process, the expectation is that interventions are required on a periodic basis.

I agree with Amuta to an extent that the decolonization experience and analysis should not call into being an automatic adoption of pre-colonial African norms as the source from which interventions should be derived. This is to assume that those norms remained unadulterated and in their pristine conditions. Yet we have to get a full understanding as to how extant culture explains several aspects of behaviors, practices, and sense of community even against the background of a massive assault from outside in the forms of evangelization, the slave trade, colonialism, and even the imposition in our time of "globalization" in hegemonic dimensions.

Conclusion

In conclusion, from the foregoing, what is strongly fostered in this paper is the role of the culture nexus construct in efforts to establish and sustain Africana Studies as a discipline. The application of the construct fuels the growth and development of Africana Studies epistemologically, theoretically, methodologically, professionally, and pedagogically. The discussion on the debate among scholars of African literature exemplifies how the construct can be seen at work.

It is not possible to present, in this work, all the debates going on in disciplines associated with Africana Studies. Kershaw (2004) identifies, for instance, two approaches that have emanated from the changes that occurred in the area of Africana Studies over the past several years: centric and scholar-activist. The culture nexus construct can be applied in diagnosing the constituent elements of the approaches identified and the interventions they represent. Suffice it to say that the debates point to the need to develop, for instance, theoretical constructs and perspectives that would assist scholars in engaging the Africana problematic in a manner that would yield results, which may bring about answers/solutions to the multifarious problems confronting Africa and its diaspora. It is precisely because of such an exigency that the argument for the utilization of the culture nexus construct is advanced here as the search continues for the epistemological, theoretical, methodological, professional, and pedagogical bases of an Africana Studies discipline.

References

Amuta, Chidi. (1989). *The Theory of African Literature.* London: Zed Books.

Burke, Kenneth. (1968). *Counter-Statement.* Berkeley, CA: University of California Press.

——.(1969). *A Rhetoric of Motives.* Berkeley, CA: University of California Press.

——.(1969). *A Grammar of Motives.* Berkeley, CA: University of California Press.

Armah, Ayi Kwei. (1968). *The Beautiful Ones Are Not Yet Born.* Boston: Houghton Mifflin.

Black, Edwin. (1965). *Rhetorical Criticism: A Study in Method.* New York: Macmillan.

Blake, Cecil A. (1993). Traditional African Values and the Right to Communicate. *Africa Media Review,* Volume 7, No. 3, December 1993, pp. 1-17.

Blake, Cecil. (1995). *Public Speaking: A Twenty-First Century Perspective.* Dubuque, IA: Kendall/Hunt Publishers.

Campbell, Kathrine Kohrs and Thomas R. Burkholder (1997) *Critiques of contemporary rhetoric.* New York: Wadsworth.

Chinweizu, Onwuchekwa Jemie and Ikechuckwu Madubuikwe. (1983). *Toward the Decolonization of African Literature.* Vol. 1. *African Fiction and Poetry and Their Critics.* Enugu: Fourth Dimension.

Golden, James L., Godwin F. Berquist and William E. Coleman. (1992). *The Rhetoric of Western Thought.* 5th Edition. Dubuque, IA: Kendall/Hunt Publishing Company.

Joko Smart, H. M. (1983). *Sierra Leone Customary Family Law.* Freetown, Sierra Leone: Fourah Bay College Bookshop Limited.

Kershaw, Terry. (2004). "Editor's comment." The *International Journal of Africana Studies.* Vol.10, #1. p. iv.

Kallsen, T.J. and D.E. McCoy. (1963). *Rhetoric and Reading: Order and Idea.* New York: Dodd, Mead & Company.

Mudumbi, V.Y. (1985). African literature: Myth or Reality. In *African Literature Studies: The Present State/L'Etat Present.* Stephen Arnold, ed. Washington, D.C.: Three Continent Press.

Owomoyela, Oyekan. (1993). *A History of Twentieth-Century African Literatures.* Lincoln, NE: University of Nebraska Press.

Peters, Jonathan. English-Language fiction from West Africa. In Soyinka, Wole. (1976). *Myth, Literature and the African World.* Cambridge: Cambridge University Press.

Owonoyela,Oyekan. *A History of Twentieth-Century African Literature.*

6

Race, Gender, and Africana Theorizing

Delores P. Aldridge

African-centered theory or Africana theory is grounded in cosmo-logical, epistemological and axiological issues, characterized by a perspective that locates Africa at its center. In the contemporary world, meaning is derived from the totality of the African's being. "African" is perceived as a "composite African," not a specific, discrete African orientation which would rather mean ethnic identification, for example, Yoruba, Ashanti, Fante, Nuba, Zulu, and so on (Asante, 1997). Just as Africana theory is grounded in cosmological, epistemological and axiological issues, race, gender, class, and culture are fundamental to understanding the issues.

Race is a social and cultural concept which embodies the dominant factors in intergroup relations in the USA. Another concept of necessity for Africana theory to be relevant is that of gender—male and female in the development of African people. Gender is crucial in explanations focusing on social, political, economic, cultural, or aesthetic dimensions of African life. In a capitalist society such as the USA, class is a salient factor for understanding a group's development. Class categorizations for the Africana theorist consist of four dimensions of property relation-ships: (1) those who possess income-producing properties; (2) those who possess some property that produces income and a job that supplements income; (3) those who maintain professions or positions because of skills; and (4) those who do not have skills and whose services may or may not be employed (Asante, 1997). Culture for an Africana theorist is a concept which contributes to explaining shared perceptions, at-titudes, and a predisposition that allow people to organize experiences in particular ways.

While it is recognized that the concepts of race, gender, class, and culture are critical to the development of Africana Studies, the major focus of this presentation is on race, gender, and to a lesser extent class and culture. No discipline can realize its full potential without recognizing the contributions and developing the talents of both genders and integrating scholarship by and about both genders. Thus, it is vital that both women and men be at the center of Africana Studies. Women are numerically and intellectually critical to the development of all that constitutes American and world scholarship. While women know this and now demand their rightful place everywhere, some men also recognize the relevance of women to the full development of the young discipline of Africana Studies and encourage their centralization. Specifically, this presentation attempts to examine the involvement of women in the development of the discipline of Africana Studies with emphasis upon women's scholarship and creative ways in which they are moving to help frame the discourse.

From the inception of the discipline of Africana Studies in America, women have been involved in its structure in departments, in regional and national organizations, and its advocacy as spokespersons through various mediums. While women writers in general have contributed significantly in developing scholarship, all too often their scholarship has focused on women rather than broader theoretical and empirical issues, which have largely been the domain of men. The following topics will be examined briefly in this discourse:

1. Early Advocacy for Engendering Africana Studies;
2. Scholarship and Research Agendas in Africana Studies;
3. Africana Women and Curriculum Development;
4. Selected Examples of Theoretical and Empirical Work;
5. Continuing Issues for Race, Gender and Africana Theorizing.

Early Advocacy for Engendering in Africana Studies

In 1984-1988, as the unprecedented two-term elected president of the National Council for Black Studies, I spearheaded dialogue on the question of placing Africana Women's Studies under Africana Studies. I had thought the issue of engendering so important as to edit a special issue on women for the *Journal of Black Studies* in 1989. And in 1992 I decided to write about gender issues in the discipline which resulted in the seminal work on "Womanist Issues in Black Studies: Toward Integrating Africana Women into Africana Studies" in the *AfroCentric*

Scholar. In this same year, I also edited a special issue of *Phylon: The Review of Race and Culture* and included an article by my former student, Beverly Guy-Sheftall entitled "Black Women's Studies: The Interfaces of Women's Studies and Black Studies."

My experiences in a leadership position at the national level and as a founding director of one of the oldest programs in the USA had provided a particular perspective that I believed worthy of documenting. Importantly, it appeared from my observations that women were debating whether to choose between Women's Studies and Black Studies academic units so that they might be central to the discourse. At the same time, the critical question became "could Black or Africana Studies be authentic without giving equal time to both the male and female gender?" This question surfaced frequently in a national survey I administered in 1992 under a Ford Foundation funded grant to the National Council for Black Studies.

In 2006, it is widely accepted that two of the most significant challenges for American higher education over the last three and a half decades have emerged from the Africana (Black Studies) and Women's Studies movements. Black or Africana Studies began as a field of study in the 1960s in the wake of the Civil Rights Movement and in the midst of pervasive campus unrest. From the outset it had both an academic and social mission. And, while contemporary Black Studies as an interdisciplinary enterprise is a product of the sixties, it draws much of its academic content from earlier times.

Students of the sixties were confronted with an absence or distortion of the black experience in the higher education curriculum and a sense of cultural alienation generated by the predominantly white colleges and universities they entered. First they demanded black recognition in any form, such as black faculty and staff, black programs, more black students, necessary financial aid, and black history courses. But, it quickly became clear that black history was simply a beginning and that a broader demand would and did emerge for a comprehensive interdisciplinary curriculum with history at its center.

Women's Studies sought to introduce the study of women as a means of providing her story and to eradicate many of the myths and distortions surrounding the lives of women. The Women's Liberation Movement, following on the heels of the Civil Rights Movement, served as a catalyst for consciousness-raising on women's issues. And, though much controversy has surrounded the movement with opposition from both men and women, whites and nonwhites, its effects have pervaded the society at all levels, including the university, where women faculty and staff have led in attempts to bring equity to gender issues. For the most part white women, benefitting from and modeling after the efforts of the Civil Rights and Black Studies Movements, have fostered an explosion of new approaches and content in the academy. Their increasing numbers and continuity have played heavily into their institutionalization in American higher education. Whereas Africana students, who are transient but in larger numbers than Africana faculty, have been a mainstay in pecking away at institutional barriers to the incorporation and perpetuation of Africana Studies, Women's Studies has enjoyed the growing critical mass of women faculty and staff with real access to structural change.

While both movements addressed some very real inadequacies, such as paucity of faculty, absence and distortion of curriculum content and programmatic resources in the academy, neither has fully incorporated African-American women scholars or the unique experiences of women of African descent in America, on the continent, and throughout the African diaspora.

Some Africana women intellectuals have viewed the struggles of women of African descent in America as part of a wider struggle for human dignity and empowerment. As early as 1893, Anna Julia Cooper in a speech to women provided this perspective:

> We take our stand on the solidarity of humanity, the oneness of life, and the un-naturalness and injustice of all special favoritisms, whether of sex, race, country, or condition.... The colored woman feels that woman's cause is one and universal; and that ... not till race, color, sex, and condition are seen as accidents, and not the substance of life, not till the universal title of humanity to life, and the pursuit of happiness is conceded to be inalienable to all, not till then is woman's lesson taught and woman's cause won—not the white woman's nor the black woman's, not the red woman's, but the cause of every man and of every woman who has writhed silently under a mighty wrong. (Loewenberg and Bogin 1976)

This humanist vision led Alice Walker, the novelist to identify with the term womanist. She defines "womanist" in *In Search of Our Mother's Gardens: Womanist Prose*. For Walker, as a womanist, is one who is "committed to the survival and wholeness of an entire people." However, her definition culminates in the problematic reference that "womanist is to feminist as purple is to lavender." Clenora Hudson-Weems (1993) takes us to another dimension in her concept of Africana womanism. The concept, Africana, perhaps, first received national visibility as a descriptor of Africana Studies with the naming of the Africana Studies and Research Center at Cornell University. In the book, *Africana Womanism: Reclaim-*

ing Ourselves, Hudson-Weems explores the dynamics of the conflict between the mainstream feminist, the Black feminist, and the Africana womanist. In this work, she names and defines traits that characterize an Africana woman. According to Hudson-Weems, Africana womanism is "neither an outgrowth nor an addendum to mainstream feminism," but rather a concept grounded in the culture, and focuses on the experiences, needs, and desires of Africana women. Africana womanists and feminists have separate agendas (p. 24). Feminism is female-centered; Africana womanism is family-centered; feminism is concerned primarily with ridding society of sexism; Africana womanism is concerned with ridding society of racism first, then classism and sexism. Many feminists say their number one enemy is the male; Africana womanists welcome and encourage male participation in their struggle. Feminism, Hudson-Weems says, is incompatible with Africana women, as it was designed to meet the needs of white women. In fact, the history of feminism reveals a blatant, racist background.

The Civil Rights Movement in America, which stressed liberation in the late sixties, marked the first time Africana people engaged in a struggle to resist racism whereby distinct boundaries were established, which separated the roles of women and men. Africana male activists publicly acknowledged expectations that women involved in the movement conform to a subservient role pattern. This sexist expectation was expressed as women were admonished to manage household needs and breed warriors for the revolution. Toni Cade (1970) elaborated on the issue of roles that prevailed in black organizations during the sixties:

> It would seem that every organization you can name has had to struggle at one time or another with seemingly mutinous cadres of women getting salty about having to man the telephones or fix the coffee while the men wrote the position papers and decided on policy. Some groups condescendingly allotted two or three slots in the executive order to women. Others encouraged the sisters to form a separate caucus and work out something that wouldn't split the organization. Others got nasty and forced the women to storm out to organize separate workshops. Over the years, things have sort of been cooled out. But I have yet to hear a coolheaded analysis of just what any particular group's stand is on the question. Invariably, I hear from some dude that Black women must be supportive and patient so that Black men can regain their manhood. The notion of womanhood, they argue—and only if pressed to address themselves to the notion do they think of it or argue—is dependent on his defining his manhood. (pp. 107-108)

While many black women activists did not succumb to the attempts of black men to reduce them to a secondary role in the movement, some did. bell hooks writes:

> Black women questioning and or rejecting a patriarchal black movement found little solace in the contemporary women's movement. For while it drew attention to the dual victimization of black women by racist and sexist oppression, white feminists tended to romanticize the black female experience rather than discuss the negative impact of oppression. When feminists acknowledge in one breath that black women are victimized and in the same breath emphasize their strength they imply that though black women are oppressed they manage to circumvent the damaging impact of oppression by being strong—and that is simply not the case. Usually, when people talk about the "strength" of black women they are referring to the way in which they perceive black women coping with oppression. They ignore the reality that to be strong in the face of oppression is not the same as overcoming oppression, that endurance is not to be confused with transformation. (1981, p. 6)

Thus, to be an activist in the liberation of black people or women did not necessarily mean there was sensitivity for Africana women.

In *All the Women Are White, All the Blacks Are Men, but Some of Us Are Brave,* three Africana women scholars wrote:

> Women's Studies ... focused almost exclusively upon the lives of white women. Black Studies, which was much too often male-dominated, also ignored Black women ... Because of white women's racism and Black men's sexism, there was no room in either area for a serious consideration of the lives of Black women. And even when they have considered Black women, white women usually have not had the capacity to analyze racial politics and Black culture, and Black men have remained blind or resistant to the implications of sexual politics in Black women's lives. (Hull, Scott, and Smith, 1981, xx-xxi)

The above characterization and concerns have seemingly been acknowledged within the last decade; there has been increasing advocacy for recognition and correction of this failure to deal equitably with Africana women in scholarship and the academy. In the revised edition of *Introduction to Black Studies* (1995), Karenga included a section on Black/Africana Women's Studies. This was the first time that a basic Africana text had devoted a section to women.

Earlier, as mentioned, I had provided the seminal work advocating the integration of Africana women into Africana Studies. Karenga stated that Black/Africana Women's Studies is a fundamental and indispensable part of the field. With the inclusion of this section, black males in the field, he encourages men to rethink their values when organizing courses and other programmatic entities of the discipline so that the unique experiences of Africana women are fully integrated into all offerings. Throughout the country Africana men and women speak to the existence of racism in Women's Studies and sexism in Africana Studies in courses on campuses, in associations, and in scholarly publications. This leads us to a discussion of scholarship and research agendas in Africana Studies.

Scholarship and Research Agendas in Africana Studies

As we focus on scholarship and research agendas, the question becomes what should be the purview of women? What research have they produced and what new directions ought they be considering? If the discipline is to include and respect them, do they need to conduct research on themselves but also in a broader arena? Within Black/Africana Studies, young scholar activists should be encouraged to focus research on issues dealing with social, political, economic, cultural, and aesthetic problems which are legitimate areas of concern for the Africana theorist. They should be encouraged to further theoretical and empirical research that is reflective of Black women's experiences, successes, sorrows, and contributions. But, women must do more than write about themselves; they must develop theories and address broader issues that are inclusive of males, families, and communities globally, nationally, and locally. And they must label their work as have men so as to be central to the discourse facilitating greater citation of their work. I contend that an Africana womanist perspective creates a space for women to be at the center of developing scholarship which may or may not have them as the specific subject matter. Put another way, women must create theoretical and empirical work that may or may not center solely or at all on their lives. Africana womanism also suggests women will be at the center of creating policies and directives that are positive for black men, women, and children.

This kind of scholarship is a creative way of integrating Africana women into African Studies in the academy. This Africana womanist perspective that I present does not worry itself with bashing white women, men or those who disagree with it. It simply seeks to empower women by putting them at the table where they may compete for an equal and pivotal space.

Black women's contributions to, and voices in, education are challenging old perspectives and adding bold, new ones in the academy. This thrust is particularly relevant to the development of Black/Africana Studies. Like other social movements, however, these women who are theorists have not necessarily enjoyed the visibility of male scholars. Who are some of these women? What have been their contributions to the discourse in the development of the discipline?

There were various pioneering works in the seventies and eighties, which included Toni Cade's *The Black Woman* (1970), the first anthology of its kind on African women in America, with its focus on the voices of Africana women themselves who analyzed contemporary issues.

In 1972 Gerda Lerner, a white historian, provided *Black Women in White America: A Documentary History* demonstrating the importance of examining the experiences of women of African descent as distinct from those of non-Africana women and Africana men. Following on the heels of these two works was the first anthology by two Africana historians, Rosalyn Terborg-Penn and Sharon Harley. Their work, *The Afro-American Woman: Struggles and Images* (1978), is a collection of original essays from a historical perspective. A single-authored historical volume by Deborah Gray White entitled *Ain't I a Woman?* (1985) provides some new insights into the lives of slave women. Earlier, a controversial, but valuable piece for illuminating the complexity of Africana womanhood was the interdisciplinary work of bell hooks' *Ain't I a Woman: Black Women and Feminism* (1981). Also, at the beginning of the decade of the eighties, several social science anthologies were developed, one, *The Black Woman* edited by LaFrances Rodgers-Rose (1980) and another, edited by Filomina Chioma Steady (1981) entitled *The Black Woman Crossculturally.* The former work by Rodgers-Rose was and remains the first edited definitive volume of original research by African-American women social scientists on African-American women. The latter volume by Steady was an outstanding accomplishment in arraying a wide range of works focusing on Africana women throughout the world.

A single-authored volume of significance in the 1980s was by Lena Wright Myers entitled *Black Women: Do They Cope Better?* This sociological work provided a new framework for understanding how women of African descent in America viewed themselves positively in spite of a racist, sexist, classist society. Another sociological work that has not received the exposure it deserves, *Black Women, Feminism and Black Liberation: Which Way?* (1985) was written by Vivian Gordon. This work places in perspective the critical issues facing Africana women and Africana Studies if the field of Africana Studies is to fully realize its potential. Aldridge (1991) authored a trailblazing work which attempted for the first time to theoretically conceptualize black male-female relationships in America. The work, *Focusing: Black Male-Female Relationships* provided a foundation for understanding relationships with strategies for developing healthy ones. Earlier in 1989, Aldridge had laid the groundwork with *Black Male-Female Relationships: A Resource Book of Selected Materials*, which was an edited volume comprising the most comprehensive collection of scholarly works available written by Africana women scholars trained with social science orientations.

Dozens of books and articles in the literary tradition were authored over the last two decades. There were also several encyclopedic volumes on Black women to emerge (Clark Hine, 1993; 2005). Of course, there were many other works of historical and literary significance written over the decades of the eighties and nineties, too numerous to note for this presentation. But, some of the books of theoretical significance developed by and about Africana women in the USA are:

1. Angela Davis, *Women, Race and Class*. New York: Random, (1981).
2. Vivian V. Gordon, *Black Women, Feminism and Black Liberation: Which Way?* Chicago: Third World Press. (1985).
3. Patricia Hill-Collins, *Black Feminist Thought: Knowledge, Conciousness, and the Politics of Empowerment*. London: Harper Collins Academic (1990).
4. Delores P. Aldridge, *Focusing: Institutional and Interpersonal Perspecitves on Black Male-Female Relationships*. Chicago: Third World Press (1991).
5. Linda Myers, *Optimal Theory and Philosophical and Academic Origins of Black Studies*. Dubuque, IA: Kendall/Hunt (1992).
6. Clenora Hudson-Weems, *Africana Womanism: Reclaiming Ourselves*. Troy, MI: Bedford Publishers, Inc. (1993).
7. Marimba Ani, *Yorugu: An African-Centered Critique of European Cultural Thought and Behavior*. Trenton, NJ: Africa World Press. (1994).
8. Kimberle Crenshaw and Kendall Thomas, *Critical Race Theory: The Key Writings that Formed the Movement*. New York: New Press (1995).
9. Clenora Hudson-Weems, *Africana Womanist Literary Theory*. Trenton, NJ: Africa World Press. (2004).

In addition to the above cited theoretical works are numerous efforts by women to participate in framing central issues of the discipline. These include Carlene Young's guest edited special issue of the *Journal of Negro Education* (1984) and three guest edited issues by Aldridge for the *Journal of Black Studies* (1989); *Phylon: Review of Race and Culture* (1992); and *Western Journal of Black Studies* (2005). In 2001, Hudson-Weems was the guest editor for a special issue on Africana Womanism for the *Western Journal for Black Studies*. Earlier, in 2000, Aldridge and Young edited *Out of the Revolution: The Development of Africana Studies,* the first time that a major text on Africana Studies had been edited by two Africana women. Thus, there has been a steady stream of scholarship including several theoretical works by women, most of whom have not received the visibility of male theorists. This lack of visibility is noteworthy because it can be observed in the curriculum and the training of the next generation of Africana scholars.

Africana Women and Curriculum Development

Presently, entrenchment in the academy, in terms of formal courses, has been far less observable than the scholarship developed over the last two decades. Significantly, the first *Core Curriculum Guide* developed by the National Council for Black Studies (1981) did not address the issue of inclusion of women as a distinct focus for study, notwithstanding theoretical work by women. Further, Colón's particularly crucial work, "Critical Issues in Black Studies: A Selective Analysis," (1984) failed to devote attention to the lack of inclusion of women in curricula in any significant way as an area of concern. These omissions were addressed a decade later in the *Revised Core Curriculum Guide* of the National Council for Black Studies and in subsequent works by visible male Africana Studies scholars as well as female Africana Studies scholars. The point is that a primary way to train developing scholars to be sensitive to inclusion of women is to have them examine their theories in the classroom. Of course, the women theorists have to be sought out and systematically included. To my knowledge there are few courses focusing on race, gender, and Africana theorizing.

A cursory examination of curricula in Africana Studies or Women's Studies(as distinct from Africana Women Studies) units reflects minimum, if any, courses that treat Africana women in their own right. And, when they do, most often the courses are in literature and occasionally tied to a family course. There are some exceptions, usually where courses are jointly listed in Africana and Women Studies with titles such as the Black Woman in America or The Black Woman in History. Notably where proactive Africana Women's scholars are located, there are generally one or two courses in the course listings.

The above tenuous assessment is based on an examination of a limited sample of schools with both Africana and Women's Studies academic units. It should also be noted that institutions that have white women scholars who are sensitive to Africana women's issues and are politically astute enough to recognize the fertile terrain for research are more likely to have courses that give attention to issues of importance for Africana women. But, it is necessary to bear in mind the struggle that exists to control curricula on Africana women as well as to gain and maintain loyalty and commitment to Africana Studies by Africana women on campuses where strong Women's Studies programs exist. In *But Some of Us Are Brave,* there are course descriptions of African-American Women's Studies. Some of these courses may prove to be useful as a point of departure for developing courses on Africana women in programs where they are nonexistent.

The first, and perhaps only, Graduate degrees (Ph.D./Masters) in English with an Africana concentration was inaugurated at the University of Missouri, Columbia in 2001. The first Ph.D. with a dissertation on Africana Womanism highlighting Africana Womanist literary theory was granted in 2006. This program was conceived by Professor Clenora Hudson-Weems in the late 1990s. It provides a model for developing similar programs at research institutions. More recently, Cornell University's Africana Studies Research Center has directed women centered institutes under the leadership of Professor James Turner. These institutes have involved senior black women scholars interfacing with junior scholars and graduate students. A central objective was/is to demonstrate creative ways of introducing Africana women's lives into curriculum. I would advocate more such nationally directed institutes and particularly in different regions of the country with emphasis on Africana women and theory construction.

There is a growing number of Africana male scholars with an interest in Africana women's issues as well as an increasing number of Africana administrators, both male and female, who are sensitive to women's issues (Franklin, 2002; Semmes, 2003) and who realize the need to incorporate significantly the curricula and experiences of students both male and female. For example, the Emory University African-American and African Studies program, under its founding Africana woman director, inaugurated an endowed lecture series in the name of an African-American woman and subsequently created a distinguished chair in the name of an Africana woman with an African-American woman as the first individual to hold the chair. Both incidents were firsts at a major institution in this country. But until recently there was lack of a strong presence of Africana women in the curriculum in this institution for a variety of reasons, including, most importantly, the lack of continuity of faculty equipped to teach these courses.

Selected Examples of Theoretical and Empirical Work

Importantly, while women build institutions via academic programs and curriculum, I cannot overemphasize the necessity for both empirical and theoretical contributions to scholarship. It is through theory and paradigm development that a discipline is framed. Thus, those who participate in this important work become central to the discipline. Both genders must participate in the framing of the discourse as well as examining and presenting subsets of it.

I have selected three examples of my own theoretical and empirical work to make the point, some of which is gender specific and which is not.

—D.P. Aldridge (1998). "Black Women and the New World Order: Toward a Fit in the Economic Marketplace."

African American women and men will face both challenges and opportunities at the dawn of the twenty-first century, which will be characterized by highly developed technology in the workplace. Any model that is designed to understand and promote the engagement of black women in the new world order must reflect the diversity of black women's historical-cultural experiences and provide an action plan. Such a model must (1) be centered in the historical- cultural experiences of black people yet meet the needs of the highly scientific and technological world of the twenty-first century; (2) focus on educational and employment equity issues at every level to maximize the potential of blacks in general—and black women specifically—in the scientific-technological professions by increasing their numbers in these areas; and (3) be action oriented so as to transform institutions and values both within and outside the black community that impede the promotion of science and technology with and for black people. In other words, a model should be African centered and have components that account for historical-cultural experiences, equity, and action for the labor market (HEAL).

—D. P. Aldridge (2000). "On Race and Culture: Beyond Afrocentrism, Eurocentrism to Cultural Democracy."

The author provides a framework for approaching and understanding the interplay of race and culture in a changing USA. She contends that the struggle for cultural democracy in American education will be critical in determining the quality and the future of education and of America itself. Cultural democracy recognizes the human right of each ethnic/cultural group in a culturally diverse society to have equal access to life chances and sources of social power. Power means to have a "voice," that is, to have the capacity to define oneself as an active participant in the world rather than a passive victim. Thus, the "voice" as expressed in the theoretical under-pinnings or major premises of Afrocentrism, Eurocentrism, and cultural democracy is examined with emphasis on their current contributions and future possibilities for shaping higher education and charting the directions in intergroup relations in American society in the twenty-first century.

—D. P. Aldridge (2001). "The Structural Components of Violence in Black Male-Female Relationships."

An Africana Lens Model provides a point of departure for the understanding of Black female-male violence. American society is defined by and derived from core or dominant values, which have differentially impacted its diverse populations. The

Africana Lens Model presented in this discourse focuses on these values as being counterproductive for black male-female relationships. Capitalism, racism, sexism and the Judeo-Christian ethic comprise the four-prong institutional or structural value components of the Africana Lens Model. This dynamic framework is instructive as it helps social scientists view domestic violence in black adult relationships from a different perspective.

The above mentioned works demonstrate the kind of work that reflects the extent of the thoughts and approaches of one Africana woman scholar with a grounding in social theory and social processes. It draws on race, gender, class, and culture to explain social, political, economic, and culture issues impacting the lives of Africana women. In doing so, it focuses on the various components crucial to Africana theorizing as pointed out at the beginning of this work. It allows focus on women, but does not restrict a reach to broader issues as has been characterized more often by the work of men. These examples are used to suggest that Africana theorizing is within the purview of Africana women.

Continuing Issues for Race, Gender and Africana Theorizing

Laverne Gyant (2000) presented findings from a study in which she conducted in-depth interviews with a selected sample of women to provide insight into their involvement in the development of Africana/Black Studies. The women in the study cited numerous issues they faced. These included defending the legitimacy of Black/Africana Studies, maintaining professional ideological beliefs, maintaining professional and personal associations, remaining inspired and motivated, and dealing with the reluctance of black males to acknowledge female contributions to the discipline. Other issues are offered for consideration to approach creatively as we move to make women central to Africana Studies theorizing and development. James Stewart (1992) advocated a number of developmental thrusts necessary for further development of the discipline. I agree with Stewart and submit that women must increasingly join men in these developmental thrusts. They are:

1. Development of a theory of history;
2. Articulation of a theory of knowledge and social change;
3. Delineation of a theory of "race" and culture;
4. Expansion of the scope of inquiry encompassed by the disciplinary matrix;
5. Expanded examination of the historical precedents to modern Africana Studies;
6. Strengthened linkages to interests outside academe to minimize misappropriation of knowledge and improve information dissemination.

If indeed women could become central to each of these thrusts from their Africana women centered perspectives, while also focusing on women's lives, then many of the concerns of women could be dealt with as Africana Studies ensures its survival and development. To be sure, a discipline can only be as strong as its theoretical foundations, the development of which is no easy task for both genders, let alone a single gender.

References

Aldridge, Delores P. "The African American Woman: Complexities in the Midst of a Simplistic World View," guest editor, *Journal of Black Studies* 20, no. 2, 1989.

———. *Black Male-Female Relationships: A Resource Book.* Dubuque, Iowa: Kendall-Hunt, 1989.

———. *Focusing: Institutional and Interpersonal Perspectives on Black Male-Female Relations.* Chicago: Third World Press, 1991.

_____ed. *New Perspectives on Black Studies*, special issue, *Phylon: Review of Race and Culture* 49, nos. 1 and 2, (spring 1992).

———. "Womanist Issues in Black Studies: Toward Integrating of Africana Women into Africana Studies," *Afrocentric Scholar* 1, no. 1, (May 1992).

———. "Black Women and the New World Order: Toward a Fit in the Economic Marketplace," In *Latinas and African American Women at Work: Race, Gender, and Economic Inequality*, Irene Browne, ed. New York: Russell Sage Foundation, 1998, pp. 357 -379.

———. "On Race and Culture: Beyond Afrocentrism, Eurocentrism to Cultural Democracy," *Sociological Focus*, Vol. 33, No. 1, (February 2000), pp. 95- 107.

———. and Carlene Young, eds., *Out of the Revolution: The Development of Africana Studies.* Lanham, MD: Lexington Books, 2000.

———. "The Structural Components of Violence in Black Male-Female Relationships," (with Willa Hemmons) *Journal of Human Behavior in the Social Environment*, Vol. 4, No. 4, 2001, pp. 209 - 226.

Ani, Marimba. *Yurungu: An African-Centered Critique of European Cultural Thought and Behavior.* Trenton, NJ: Africa World Press, Inc., 1994.

Asante, Molefe. "Afrocentricity and the Quest for Method," in James Conyers, ed. *Africana Studies: A Disciplinary Quest for Both Theory and Method.* Jefferson, NC: McFarland & Co., 1997.

Bell, Roseann P., Bettye J. Parker, and Beverly Guy-Sheftall, eds. *Sturdy Black Bridges: Visions of Black Women in Literature.* New York: Anchor Books, 1979.

Cade, Toni, ed., *The Black Woman: An Anthology.* New York: New American Library, 1970.

Collins, Patricia H. *Black Feminist Thought: Knowledge, Consciousness, and the Politics of Empowerment.* London: Harper Collins Academic, 1990.

Cólon, Alan K. "Critical Issues in Black Studies: A Selective Analysis," *Journal of Negro Education* 53 (1984), 268-277.

Crenshaw, Kimberle and Kendall Thomas. *Critical Race Theory: The Key Writings that Formed the Movement.* New York: New Press, 1995.

Davis, Angela. *Women, Race and Class.* New York: Random, 1981.

Franklin, V. P. (2002). "Hidden in Plain View: African American Women, Radical Feminism, and the Origins of Women's Studies Programs, 1967 - 1974," *The Journal of African American History*, Vol. 87, (Fall): 433 - 445.

Gordon, Vivian V. *Black Women, Feminism, and Black Liberation: Which Way?* Chicago: Third World Press, 1985.

———. "The Coming of Age of Black Studies," *Western Journal of Black Studies* 5, no. 3 (fall 1981).

Gregory, Sheila T. *Black Women in the Academy: the Secret to Success and Achievement.* New York: University Press of America, 1995.

Gyant, Laverne, "The Missing Link: Women in Black/Africana Studies." In *Out of the Revolution: The Development of Africana Studies*, Delores P. Aldridge and Carlene Young, eds. Lanham, MD: Lexington Books, 2000, pp. 177-189.

Harley, Sharon, and Rosalyn Terborg-Penn, eds., *The Afro-American Woman: Struggles and Images.* Port Washington, NY: Kennikat Press, 1978.

Hine, Darlene Clark. *Black Women in America: An Historical Encyclopedia.* Brooklyn, NY: Carlson Publishing, 1993.(Revised Edition, New York: Oxford University Press, 2005).

hooks, bell. *Ain't I A Woman: Black Women and Feminism.* Boston: South End Press, 1981.

Hudson-Weems, Clenora. *Africana Womanism: Reclaiming Ourselves.* Troy, MI: Bedford Publishers, Inc., 1993.

———. Guest Editor, *Africana Womanism,* Special Issue, *Western Journal of Black Studies,* Vol. 25, No.3, Fall, 2001.

———.*Africana Womanist Literary Theory.* Trenton, NJ: Africa World Press, 2004.

Hull, Gloria T., Patricia Bell Scott, and Barbara Smith, eds. *All the Women Are White, All the Men Are Black, but Some of Us Are Brave: Black Women's Studies.* Old Westbury, NY: The Feminist Press, 1982.

Karenga, Maulana. *Introduction of Black Studies.* Revised Edition. Los Angeles, CA: University of Sankore Press, 1995.

Lerner, Gerda, ed. *Black Women in White America: A Documentary History.* New York: Pantheon Books, 1972.

Loewenberg, Bert J. and Ruth Bogin, eds. *Black Women in Nineteenth-Century American Life.* University Park: Pennsylvania State Press, 1976.

Myers, Lena W. *Black Women: Do They Cope Better?* New York: Prentice-Hall, 1980.

Myers, Linda J. *Optimal Theory and Philosophic and Academic Origins of Black Studies.* Dubuque, Iowa: Kendall/Hunt, 1992.

National Council for Black Studies. *Black Studies Core Curriculum.* Bloomington, IN: National Council for Black Studies, 1981.

Rodgers-Rose, LaFrances. *The Black Woman.* Beverly Hills, CA: Sage Publications, 1980.

Semmes, Clovis. *Cultural Hegemony and African American Development.* Westport, CT: Praeger, 1992.

Steady, Filomina ed. *The Black Woman Cross-Culturally.* Cambridge, MA: Schenkman Publishing Co., 1981.

Stewart, James B. (1992). "Reaching for Higher Ground: Toward an Understanding of Black Africana Studies," *The Afrocentric Scholar*, 1, 1-63.

Walker, Alice. *The Color Purple.* New York: Washington Square Press, 1982.

———. *In Search of Our Mother's Gardens: Womanist Prose.* New York: Harcourt Brace, Jovanovich, 1983.

White, Deborah Gray. *Ain't I A Woman? Female Slaves in the Plantation South.* New York: W. W. Norton, 1985.

Young, Carlene, Guest Editor. *An Assessment of Black Studies Programs in American Higher Education,* special issue of *Journal of Negro Education* 53 (1984).

7

Must Revolutionaries Sing the Blues?: Thinking through Fanon and the Leitmotif of the Black Arts Movement

Lewis R. Gordon

"Thus the blues—'the black slave lament'—was offered up for the admiration of the oppressors. This modicum of stylized oppression is the exploiter's and the racist's rightful due. Without oppression and without racism you have no blues. The end of racism would sound the knell of great Negro music. . . . As the all-too-famous Toynbee might say, the blues are the slave's response to the challenge of oppression. Still today, for many men, even colored, Armstrong's music has a real meaning only in this perspective.

Racism bloats and disfigures the face of the culture that practices it. Literature, the plastic arts, songs for shopgirls, proverbs, habits, patterns, whether they set out to attack it or to vulgarize it, restore racism."

———*Frantz Fanon*

"Man cannot live in a valueless world."

———*Alain Locke*

Frantz Fanon, whose revolutionary reflections on social change and the human condition greatly influenced many of the artists of the Black Arts Movement, didn't like the blues. The radical change of building new concepts and setting the material infrastructure for a new humanity entails, for him, as we see in the first epigraph, a carillon call for its death. Yet, we must wonder, what would the Black Arts Movement be without the blues? Must, also, the blues be characterized as so symbiotically linked to racial oppression and resistance that the path of a negative moment in a historical dialectical battle for freedom is its only epithet?

Let us explore these questions in several parts, first, through rethinking revolution as a category of reflection in our times, and then, through the tension and expectations in the relationship between aesthetic production and material production.

I

To talk about revolutionaries in the contemporary climate often carries a tinge of nostalgia, which is awfully ironic since the whole point of a revolutionary consciousness—at least a progressive one—is to look forward. The nostalgia of revolution in conservative times exemplifies a spirit caught in the winds of an enveloping mood, where even moving forward is understood in backward terms. Such are our times; suffering, as it is, a declining public sphere, the human condition finds itself punctuated, increasingly, by resources of force and imaginative acts that wreak of a retreat from reality instead of an exploration of its possibilities. The question of revolution is, after all, one of radical social change, but making the social world change carries with it the two horns of consequence on what we are and what we ought to become. Such is the strange dualism of an epoch marked by suffering and expectations of material redemption.

The path of material redemption has received its classic formulation in the thought of Max Weber.[1] The process of modernization carries with it, however, multiple teleological promises, as also observed by Weber as "polytheistic," among which is the claim of secularization. Such a path promises a move from religious-ethical demands on lived reality to a near imperial ascent of the reach of law. Yet, the hopes of legalization as the manifestation of modern conquest of the social world brings with it accompanying limits. The gravity that underlies the concept of law in the physical world haunts such avowed sedimentation of the social world; created by human actions, it faces its demise through such agency. The social world is not, however, one simply of rationalization and control. It is also premised upon directed activities whose exhaustion is beyond morality and law and stand, instead, in upward and downward poles of faith and lived-experience of beauty and ugliness—the world, that is, of value.[2]

The problem of value, particularly in its aesthetic form, in the modern world is that it resists the completeness of rational colonization. That values are also practices of assessment requires, in a paradoxically "logical" way, that even the source of valuing logic must be beyond logic itself. One brings value to one's practices, even, as Friedrich Nietzsche has shown, to one's values.[3] This transcending capacity of values has occasioned many great expectations for their role in processes of social transformation. For colonization practices to continue, the assertion of systemic control must include a value that is an anti-value, one that attacks the conditions by which values could emerge in the first place. The source of such a value is most explicit in Medieval thought, although its roots are ancient.[4] It reverberates into the present with the familiar phrase, "God's will." In a world governed by the will of an omniscient, omnipotent, and all-just god, we find ourselves constantly in the face of human limits. What we see as unjust could be a function of our own finitude. An infinite being could see the ultimate justice in what at first appears to be unjust. This rationalization is known as theodicy. It means, literally, God's justice. If God's work is perfect and inherently just, then there are at least two accounts of evil available to us: (1) there is ultimately no evil in the world, only its appearance, and (2) evil emerges in the world as a consequence of human freedom, which makes God's complete goodness compatible with the reality of evil. On both accounts, the notion of evil is extraneous to God. What, however, should we conclude about a world that is both devoid of God and unjust? How should we account for injustice and suffering in the modern world? Here, too, we have a variety of accounts, of which we could consider two: (1) there is ultimately no injustice in the world (although there is suffering) because justice is a value and values are not, in the end, "real" or "objective"; they are simply an expression of human beings' determined points of view on the world and are often irrational, or (2) well-organized systems of knowledge and social regulations should not be blamed for the proclivities of bad people. We find, in these accounts, a secularized version of the theocentric model in the form of a system-centric model.

The system-centric model occasions reflection on the enduring grammar of idolatry and the ascription of that which is evil, unjust, and ugly to things inassimilable. Theodicy, in other words, can ironically continue through modern aspirations to the secular in the form of secularism. This move leads to new forms of rationalizations while maintaining very old legitimating forms. God is replaced by new systemic markers, and we find "science" and "political system" to be two instances of such rationalizations. With science, the move is epistemic. It becomes the ultimate source of rigor in systematic productions of knowledge. With a political system, the result is, as W.E.B. DuBois has shown in *The Souls of Black Folk*, the production of "problem people."[5] Both are consequences of systems lived as complete and closed. Their contradictions must be "outside."

It is no accident, then, that revolutionaries face a peculiar theodicean battle. They must unveil the contradictions of the system (epistemological and political) as internal, which leads to the revelation of the need for alternatives. The result is, then, a doubled-relation to the normative practices of the societies in which they live. They must both see the society as it sees itself and, literally, see the way it really is, see its contradictions. For revolutionaries, their society has a narcissistic feature of seeking self-deceiving reflections. The revolutionary's job—at least that of the revolutionary intellectuals (which includes artists)—is to eliminate such narcissism and enable their society to respond to its contradictions, to, in effect, become what that society has lived up to such a point as a misguided notion of such an event marking the end of the world.

This language of doubling and double-envisioning brings to the fore an insight from W.E.B. DuBois. Implicit in his observation of double consciousness is the accusation of hidden contradictions of American society that are lived each day by its pariah. How could justice be reconciled as separate but purportedly equal?

II

The resources available for the unveiling of societal contradictions are manifold. Although the world of prose offers theoretical reflection, such an effort also requires the force of sight and feeling. DuBois, for instance, integrated the poetic and spiritual resources in his effort to articulate the souls of black people. Similar paths were taken by Phyllis Wheatley, Martin Delany, Frederick Douglass, and Anna Julia Cooper, to name a few. In many ways, there has always been an argument brewing for a Black Arts Movement. From the moment collectives of black people began to reflect on the importance of art in struggles against slavery and racism, a particular form of argument began to take its course. We know of the importance of music and dance and the body as canvas for worship and war.[6] We also know of the importance of aesthetic production in the exploration of the horizons of black identity during the Harlem Renaissance. We also know of the unyielding body of music, dance, paintings, sculptors, literatures, and (most limited by way of resources and access) film in constructing the poetics of black identity in the period between 1930 and the late 1950s. It is in the 1960s, however, where the notion of a Black Arts Movement and Black Aesthetics became most explicit that the question of the relationship between politics and art also came to the fore. It was difficult not to see, for example, that for the group of writers in Addison Gayle's classic anthology *The Black Aesthetic* (1971), art could not be defended for its own sake to people who so desperately demanded social change, especially in the form of Black Power.[7] For them, there was a kind of artistic dimension to Marx's famous eleventh thesis on Feuerbach: the point is to change the world.

The Black Arts Movement was announcing, then, a fusion of the political and the aesthetic. The full range of aesthetic activity from artistic production to food and sex called for political assessment. We should bear in mind, however, that a rarely expressed dynamic of the other way round also emerged: the political also began to receive aesthetic markers of legitimation. How one appeared politically—from dashikis and afros to the intonation of speech—began to receive aesthetic in addition to moral appeals as the expression of Black Power. Think of the uniforms of the Black Panthers, the connections with West Africa that marked the fashion foundations of contemporary Afrocentricity, and the ever symbolic black fist raised high and mighty. Or think of the knitted caps and yarmulkes and aromatic incense of the inner-city revolutionary who exemplified a Black Muslim aesthetic.

III

Although the political dimensions of African-American artistic production are well-known, and although the classic interpretive techniques of modernism versus avant garde, formalism and surrealism, and so forth, have been utilized in the interpretation and assessment of such production, an aspect that is not often discussed, but is crucial for addressing Fanon's seemingly archaeological challenge, is the existential dimension of producing work in black. This is the case not only because of Fanon's own existential predilections, but also because of the peculiar set of existential problematics posed by the weight of European modernity on black souls, including the forms of alienation that mark modern life in both its masked and unveiled contradictions.

The word "existence" has its roots in the Latin words ex sistere, which means to stand out, to emerge, to appear. A feature of modern European life has been the suppression of many of its subjects to the point of near (although with an aim for complete) social invisibility. To exist, then, means to stand out, to become, among other things, visible. For black folks, there is a paradox here. For, as is well-known, blacks face problems of hypervisibility. The paradox is that hypervisibility is a form of invisibility. For to be hypervisible is to be seen, but to be seen in a way that crushes the self under the weight of a projected, alien self.[8] We can call this phenomenon epistemic closure. It means to be seen in a way that closes off the process of inquiry and understanding, to be seen without being seen, to be encountered without the modalities of interrogatives, to be "known" as "nothing more to know." Because existence entails emergence, such a perspective on the human condition entails a thesis of openness. The human being, in other words, is always a possibility beyond his or her immediate sedimentations or claims of permanence and fixedness. More, the human being, because of such fundamental incompleteness, creates frameworks of collective activities that eventually meet in the form of a social world. Such a world is the framework of meaning that transcends, often, the intentions of individual human beings who live such structures. In effect, human beings encounter their reflections as projections (the effect side of projects), and these projections take many forms, aesthetic productions being a set of them.

To read aesthetic productions with an eye for their existential dimensions means, then, to examine the ways in which forms of humanity appear as symbol and meaning. Why symbol and meaning? Because although a consequence of human activity (what Hannah Arendt calls work, that is, world-creating activity), the creation points in a variety of directions that transcend itself.[9] It "points" to having a creator, and thus works as a constructed and artefactual reality, and then "points" to its own realms of significations, as do most signs. Think of the etymology of "symbol," in the Greek words syn (together) and ballein (thrown). An existential analysis poses the problem of emergence, further, as a distancing of self from self. In other words, the posing of existential questions inward leads to a displacement of self that leads to the elusiveness of self. Meaning, thus, shifts from its ordinary law-like structure as we find in lexicographical meanings (which has its roots in Greek words that refer, ironically, to speech and words—for example, lexis and subsequently in Latin lex for what we now know as law) to a new, lived reality of making life meaningful; to have a meaning and to be meaningful is a distinction that brings to the fore the "given" in the former and agency in the latter. It is this link between meaningfulness and agency that stimulated another existential distinction, one between liberty (unencumbered movement) and freedom. That freedom requires the ability to raise the question of the absence of meaningful liberty and reveals the importance of the imagination in the human condition. What would life be were human beings incapable of imagination? Is not even happiness haunted by the possibility of living a dream and unhappiness the hope of only living a nightmare from which, one day, to arise through an imagined alternative? This is not to say that existence, freedom, calls for delusion. The whole point is that in our struggles with reality, we simultaneously, as Sigmund Freud observed, "daydream."[10] And just as implicit in children's daydreaming is the desire to be adults, in adult daydreaming there is, too, an ironic maturation process of transcending too much seriousness. There needs, in other words, to be possibility for life to live.

The preceding reflections abound in black existential texts. Because there is not enough space available for me to present a detailed account, consider this summary. Although we could find existential themes in African-American aesthetic productions from the nineteenth century, it is without question that Richard Wright offered the first explicit forms of existential productions in black. In *Native Son*, many of the themes of struggling for freedom, of experiencing human displacement, emerge. In his creation of the Bigger Thomas antihero, Wright introduced the black existential motif of "the racial monster," although the grammar for monstrosity in the modern world was already set down by Mary Shelley in her epochal novel *Frankenstein or the Modern Prometheus*.[11] The classic, Shelleyan monster sought recognition from his modern scientific creator who has abandoned him, and in the process of seeking companionship (a female monster) destroys his symbolic mother (his creator's wife). The racialized version, D.W. Griffith's *Birth of a Nation* (1915), has the "monsters" of American slavery attempt to destroy the white nation politically and biologically (through attempted rape of white women) and, in a transformation of Shelley's depiction of a cold, inhuman whiteness in the polar ice caps, created a fiery whiteness in ghostly Ku Klux Klan robes and hoods as the white nation's salvation. Wright, however, places an existential twist that brings Mary Shelley's insight back to the fore by looking at modernity from the monster's point of view. His thesis in *Native Son*, that the structure of American society is such that meaningful freedom is often posed against it, and for some communities can only be posed against it, where the native son of American society is Bigger Thomas, raises the question of the suspension of white normativity as a frightening aspect of a society so invested in it.[12] The ongoing motif of the black monster is that his or her innocence is, ultimately, irrelevant, which leads to a haunting innocence. Such a theme returns in Wright's

The Outsider in the character of Cross Damon, and we see it taken up in the guiding theme of invisibility in Ralph Ellison's *Invisible Man*, where public insanity is one of the few means of asserting freedom for sane and educated blacks.[13] There is, in other words, an inversion of reality that places chains on dynamics of black emergence.

Such themes are taken to more explicit aesthetic reflection in Toni Morrison's *The Bluest Eye*.[14] As Gary Schwartz pointed out in his insightful essay, "Toni Morrison at the Movies," one of the consequences of chaining black emergence is the motif of imitation.[15] To be an imitation is to be without a standard of one's own. The original, the prototype, becomes the generator of value, and thus an analytic of inferiority is always implicit. Morrison's exploration of imitation at the heart of racialized questions of beauty, with the imitation always having an analytic of less-than on a slippery slope to the ugly, with the mixed suffering the displacement of incoherence (look at the ugliness of generational incestuous mixture in the form of adult's and children's language at the beginning of the text), brings to the fore the limits of dialectics of recognition. To be as another's standard of value is to be submerged and, consequently, not to appear except as alien, even to one's self. Of course, part of the lie of blackness as imitation is that original black productions are imitated by whites to the point of Americanness, in truth, really being a creolization of black, white—and, for that matter, brown, yellow, and red. We see here a return of DuBois's theme of double consciousness, for the originality of black aesthetic production is lived as the contradiction of white normativity but is imitated by the white mainstream as a denied originality.

The existential and the meaningful raises the question of what we shall call semiotic resistance. Implicit in signs and symbols is their displacement, their always pointing beyond themselves. Meditations on freedom often take symbolic form precisely because of the always beyond yet reclaiming status of existence and values. Although Morrison's *The Bluest Eye* appeared after the emergence of the Black Arts Movement of the 1960s, it was the culmination of a set of existential reflections that lay bare the folly of the dialectics of white recognition. Just as the afro and the black fist signaled only violence for the white world, just as "Say it loud: 'I'm Black and I'm Proud!'" meant "I'm Black and I am Dangerous," the bloated and disfigured face of which Fanon wrote found itself needing to look inward, not for the sake of escape, but for the reclamation of agency through which to construct different epistemic and aesthetic conditions for that much-needed new humanity. The problem, however, is that this move manifested itself politically—that is, outwardly—which means that however inward one's search for self-love and against self-loathing might be, it goes nowhere if it makes one cease to be actional.

IV

There is no point in talking about the political without addressing what it means to be actional. In the introduction to *Black Skin, White Masks*, Fanon announced that he wanted to find a way for blacks to become actional.[16] He argued that this was needed because of the impact of overly structural (phylogenetic) and individualist (ontogenetic) accounts of the limits on black existence. Between both, he argued, are things created by a social world (sociogenetic) that, we should be reminded, unlike biochemical processes, require human beings for its continued existence. Fanon, in effect, calls for revolution because he calls for changing the social world.

Fanon is not, however, naive. He realizes that the kind of changes he is calling for is tantamount to calling for a second death of God. For the contemporary world has its own idols on whose shoulders stand the value system of racial oppression and colonialism. The transformations he is calling for require, as well, then, the critical unmasking of theodicean dynamics. The familiar DuBoisian motif of "problem people," of contradictions of a system that avows its own completeness, returns. In *Black Skin, White Masks*, Fanon reveals this through unmasking the folly of the dialectics of recognition in the delusions of linguistic mastery, white love as a source of legitimation, and, more germane to essay, the poetics of negritude. For Fanon, as for many of the artists of the later Black Arts Movement, negritude offered a form of poetic salvation. It offered a way to love blackness and, thus, love himself. But, as he learned from Jean-Paul Sartre's "Black Orpheus," such a retreat required an absolute conviction in order not to collapse into the relativism of a negative moment that recentered European humanity.[17] Loving blackness against whiteness has the reactionary effect of reinforcing whiteness. In Fanon's words, "I needed not to know." Later on, in *A Dying Colonialism*, Fanon takes heed in the positive dimension of negritude as that which was created by blacks, as an exemplar of black agency.[18] But at the end of being robbed of his "last chance" in the fifth chapter of *Black Skin, White Masks*, Fanon began to weep and wash away the narcissistic impediments to his confrontation with white social reality. It is then that he is able to explore the psychopathological dimensions of antiblack racism, and it is there that he sees clearly that the world created by European modernity lacks the concept of a normal black adult. This is because whether in the direction of the black outcast, the criminal, or in the direction of the "assimilated black subject," both have blackness and normality in opposition. The former is an accepted intersection (black and criminal have been conjoined into "black=criminal" into "black/criminal") and the latter is elimination (black does not equal normal/white; thus, assimilation = white/normal, which means "the assimilated black" is "the black who is not black," which makes contradictory the mode of being for such a figure). How can blacks be liberated by developing a healthy self identity if our identity is locked in the category of abnormality?

In his subsequent essay, "Racism and Culture," and his books *A Dying Colonialism* and *The Wretched of the Earth*, Fanon explores the question of cultural resistance and social transformation that brings to the fore the role of aesthetics broadly understood.[19] In all these texts, the leitmotif of tragic drama is set in classic fashion of competing notions of rights. There is the colonizer's "right" over all that has been colonized, and there is the colonized's "right" to fight against colonization and reclaim his or her humanity. The problem is exacerbated by the agents of struggle not often having been those at the original moment of constructing the colonial state. They are, in other words, born into the colonial condition. Such a reciprocal face-off of relative claims suspends ethical dictates without prior political resolutions. And in a world in which ethics has been suspended, what could one expect but violence to be the consequence?

That these texts are brilliant instances of a symbiosis of the poetic and the historical, as Paget Henry has shown in *Caliban's Reason*, reveals their message to the politicization of art as exemplified by the Black Arts Movement.[20] Particularly prescient, but often overlooked, is Fanon's argument in *The Wretched of the Earth*, that national consciousness must supervene over nationalism. National consciousness is the realization that a nation must be built. Nationalism is the attachment to identities that carry dangers of collapsing into ethnocentrism, tribalism, and racism. The former is an inclusive "we" that includes even responsibility of building a world for subsequent generations; the latter is always an "us versus them": "The consciousness of self is not the closing of a door to communication. Philosophic thought teaches us, on the contrary, that it is its guarantee. National consciousness, which is not nationalism, is the only thing that will give us an international dimension."[21]

The existential dimension of Fanon's thought comes to the fore here in his discussion of the role of cultural production in relation to social transformation. He argues, in effect, that existence precedes essence by arguing for the art to come out of struggles instead of art being created as conditions for struggle: "If man is known by his acts, then we will say that the most urgent thing today for the intellectual [also read as artist] is to build up his nation. If this building up is true, that is to say if it interprets the manifest will of the people and reveals the eager African peoples, then the building of a nation is of necessity accompanied by the discovery and encouragement of universalizing values."[22] At this point, Fanon would appear in opposition to the Black Arts Movement precisely because much of it was premised on black nationalism instead of the question of national consciousness. The conclusion would, however, be incorrect. Observe: "A frequent mistake, and one which is moreover hardly justifiable, is to try to find cultural expressions for and to give new values to native culture within the framework of colonial domination. This is why we arrive at a proposition which at first sight seems paradoxical: the fact that in a colonized country the most elementary, most savage, and the most undifferentiated nationalism is the most fervent and efficient means of defending national cultures" (*Wretched*, 244). Fanon's argument suggests that we should take seriously the fact that the Black Arts Movement emerged in a racist country, a country whose antiblack values so permeate its institutions that the cohesiveness offered by Black Nationalism becomes a necessary condition for the formation of the infrastructures through which struggles can emerge for the decolonizing practices that will raise the question of national consciousness versus nationalism. Put differently: the people must be in a position to build their nation for such a problematic to be meaningful. The question of decolonization as a condition for this postcolonial move is vital. And we see here a more positive reassertion of the dialectical elements that led to his earlier resolve to weep.

In these discussions, Fanon offers some insights on what could be called the semiotic moment of art in the formation of national consciousness. For without the development of new modes of expressing nationhood, old forms of identities will reign as the foundations of national identity. Although Fanon mentions a variety of artistic practices, poetry is, without question, the most privileged activity for him and many whose black revolutionary imagination was first stimulated by negritude. This would explain why, although he is critical of negritude, Fanon is especially critical of the blues. For he sees the blues as being more linked to the underlying condition of white oppression, which stimulates the worst of the reflection of white desire. The epigraphical indictment returns in more generalized form: "To believe it is possible to create black culture is to forget that niggers are disappearing just as those people who brought them into being are seeing the breakup of their economic and cultural supremacy" (234). History has not borne out this observation, given the emergence of neoliberal globalism, but the argument still holds so long as we lay claim to a necessary linkage to the continued creation of "niggers" by New World orders of racist exploitation. The argument itself rests on functionalist's foundations, where aesthetic productions have well-defined roles to play, and these roles are not assessable in aesthetic but political terms. From this point of view, the defense of centering poetry is its link to writing and speech and hence to intellectuals who are not artists. In ways, it is affirmation of the value of the word over the moan and the kinetic revolt of dance.

Is this assessment of the blues, and by extension black arts, sustainable?

V

Fanon's reflections on racism and colonialism and his observation of the absence of normality in the study of black psychopathology leads to the question of the meaning of health. For in the absence of ethical foundations, what he calls in *Wretched* the "Graeco-Latin pedestal," justice, too, has to fall sway to the reorganization of social forces for its possibility. Thus, in the absence of even the possibility of justice is left the reflection on what it means to be healthy.

Here, I should like to enlist Friedrich Nietzsche's theory of social health, which underlies, in his early work, his theory of ancient Greek tragedy. For Nietzsche health should not be interpreted as an absence of disease or adversity. It should be understood as an organism's or agent's or community's ability to deal with such travails through an affirmation of life. In *The Birth of Tragedy from the Spirit of Music*, Nietzsche argued that the ancient Greeks responded to life's misfortunes through the creation of tragic drama. This response first took form in music and the chorus and eventually gave way to more dialogue and the emergence of the hero. The hero, however, was afforded no respite through pleas of innocence, because in tragedy it is the reconciliation of opposing forces—one, Dionysian (god of music, fluids, intoxication, women, and drama) and the other, Apollonian (god of plastic arts, order, harmony, form, masculine beauty)—with different periods of emphasis but in each instance an understanding that life offers suffering, however good our souls may be. Nietzsche adds to this view of tragedy a theory of decadence, where as life decays, so, too, do its values, which often take nihilistic forms. During periods of growth, however, there is the vibrant affirmation of life.

Nietzsche could very well be describing the plight of black people in the modern world and the aesthetic response, the blues, that has emerged from such suffering. But in stream with Nietzsche's reflections on the ancient Greeks, we should question the wisdom of reducing black suffering only to racism and colonialism. Black people do not, after all, live only through such terms. There are times when the situatedness of life itself intervenes, and it is often those aspects of life that are sung about in blues music, lamented on in blues poetry, and underlie the blues aspects of the performing and visual arts. The blues is, thus, not only an aesthetics of racism but also the leitmotif of everyday life under modernity. As Ralph Ellison reflects in his poignant essay, "Richard Wright's Blues":

> The blues is an impulse to keep the painful details and episodes of a brutal experience alive in one's aching consciousness, to finger its jagged grain, and to transcend it, not by the consolation of philosophy but by squeezing from it a near-tragic, near-comic lyricism. As a form, the blues is an autobiographical chronicle of personal catastrophe expressed lyrically.[23]

That the blues should not be reduced only to racism suggests a broader role for the blues. The blues is about dealing with life's suffering of any kind. Because of this, it has become the leitmotif of modernity itself. We need only think through the many musical manifestations of the blues that have permeated the twentieth century and continue into the twenty-first: swing, jazz, rhythm and blues, soul, rock n' roll, salsa, samba, rock steady, calypso, samba, and now, hip hop. Moreover, there are aspects of the blues that exemplify its own aesthetic sensibility. Blues music is full of irony. Its sadness exemplifies an adult understanding of life that is both sober and, ironically, happy. It is a nondelusional happiness; the kind of happiness that is a realization instead of a diversion. It is the beauty of moonlight versus sunshine, although the blues dimensions of a sunny day can be understood through our realization of how much can be hidden in plain sight. Think of the numbness one seeks from alcohol and the realization offered by the blues, that numbness gets us nowhere. All blues productions remind us that life is not something to escape but something to confront. And it does so in its very form. The classical blues structure is full of repetitions, for instance, that reveal new layers of meaning about the cyclicality of life. And in this structure, although a story is retold, it is understood at different levels the effect of which is cathartic and after which is a renewed understanding of the point of origin.

The irony here is that Fanon's *Black Skin, White Masks* fits the structural description of the blues at the end of the previous paragraph. In that work, Fanon tells a story that is retold in mounting layers of revelation. At the moment of catharsis—the weeping—the sobriety offers confrontation with a reality that was too much to bear at the outset, reality without hope of normative approval, a reality in which the dialectics of recognition must be abandoned.

VI

Many of the writers of the Black Arts Movement would agree with Fanon that "every generation must out of relative obscurity discover its mission, fulfill it, or betray it" (*Wretched*, 206). Many such as Leroi Jones/Amiri Baraka, Sonia Sanchez, Nikki Giovanni, Ed Bullins, Harold Cruse, Ray Durem, Adrienne Kennedy, and Larry Neal would agree that for their generation, it meant empowering members of their community with aesthetic productions that brought both a healthy confrontation with the vicissitudes of life and a liberated consciousness whose imagination was freed to consider future possibilities. In effect, the task of constructing a livable world—a genuinely mature one—was a correlative goal. The assessment of the successes and failures of the artists of the Black Arts Movement should be considered in terms of the limitations of art itself as a medium of social change. After all, it may be the case that to demand that art change the world may be to demand too much of art. For how much can art remain art when it ceases to affect us at the level of how we feel, and how politically transformative can the stimulation of affect be by itself? This is not to say that the aesthetic realm isn't important. My argument throughout has been that it is a viable dimension of transforming inhabited spaces into livable places. It is, in other words, part of how human beings live.

Revolutionaries, those guiding luminaries that served as teleological impetus for the Black Arts Movement, must, then, sing the blues because their goal is the understanding and transformation of life. How well those artists did sing the blues is a matter for another essay. For now, it is important that they sang the blues at all and brought to consciousness that not all important battles need be those that we have won.

So we close where we began, with our epigraph from Alain Locke now as a very short epilogue: "Man cannot live in a valueless world."[24]

Notes

1. See *The Protestant Work Ethic and the Spirit of Capitalism in The Protestant Ethic and the "Spirit" of Capitalism and Other Writings*, ed, trans., and with an intro. by Peter Baehr and Gordon C. Wells (New York: Penguin Books, 2000).

2. See Alain Locke's "Values and Imperatives" in *The Philosophy of Alain Locke: Harlem Renaissance and Beyond,* ed. by Leonard Harris (Philadelphia: Temple University Press, 1989) and Søren Kierkegaard, *Either/Or,* ed. and trans. with introduction and notes by Howard V. Hong and Edna H. Hong (Princeton, NJ: Princeton University Press, 1987).

3. See, e.g., *The Will to Power*, trans. Walter Kaufmann and R. J. Hollingdale, edited, with commentary, by Walter Kaufmann, with facsimiles. of the original manuscript (New York: Random House 1967).

4. For discussion, see John Hicks's *Evil and the God of Love*, Rev. ed. (New York : Harper & Row, 1978).

5. W.E.B. DuBois, *The Souls of Black Folk*, with introductions by Nathan Hare and Alvin F. Poussaint, revised and updated bibliography (New York: Signet Classic/New American Library, 1969), 43–44.

6. E.g., the Haitian Revolution. See Michel-Rolph Trouillot, *Silencing the Past: Power and the Production of History* (Boston: Beacon Press, 1995); Joan Dyan, *Haiti, History, and the Gods* (Berkeley, CA : University of California Press, 1995); and Sibylle Fischer, *Modernity Disavowed: Haiti and the Cultures of Slavery in the Age of Revolution* (Durham: Duke University Press, 2004).

7. Addison Gayle, ed., *The Black Aesthetic* (Garden City, NY: Doubleday Publishers, 1971).

8. For discussion, see Lewis R. Gordon, *Bad Faith and Antiblack Racism* (Amherst, NY: Humanity Books, 1995/1999) and chapter 3 of Lewis R. Gordon, *Fanon and the Crisis of European Man: An Essay on Philosophy and the Human Sciences* (New York: Routledge, 1995).

9. See Hannah Arendt, *The Human Condition* (Chicago: University of Chicago Press, 1958).

10. Sigmund Freud, "The Relation of the Poet to Day-Dreaming," in *Character and Culture*, with an introduction by Philip Rieff (New York: Collier Books, 1963), especially p. 36.

11. Mary Wollstonecraft Shelley, *Frankenstein: Complete, Authoritative Text with Biographical, Historical, and Cultural Contexts, Critical History, and Essays from Contemporary Critical Perspectives*, 2nd edition, ed. by Johanna M. Smith, (Boston: Bedford/St. Martin's, 2000).

12. Richard Wright, *Native Son*, with an introduction by Arnold Rampersad (New York: HarperPerennial, 1998).

13. Richard Wright, *The Outsider*, with an introduction by Maryemma Graham (New York: Perennial, 2003) and Ralph Ellison, *Invisible Man* (New York: Vintage, 1972).

14. Toni Morrison, *The Bluest Eye* (New York: Washington Square Press, 1972).

15. Gary Schwartz, "Toni Morrison at the Movies: Theorizing Race Through Imitation of Life (for Barbara Siegel)," in *Existence in Black: An Anthology of Black Existential Philosophy*, ed. with an intro. by Lewis R. Gordon (New York: Routledge, 1997), 111–128.

16. Frantz Fanon, *Black Skin, White Masks*, trans. Charles Lam Markmann (New York: Grove Press, 1967).

17.   See Jean-Paul Sartre, "Black Orpheus," in *"What Is Literature?" and Other Essays*, intro. by Steven Unger (Cambridge, MA: Harvard University Press, 1988), 289–232.

18.   Frantz Fanon, *A Dying Colonialism*, trans. Haakon Chevalier, with an introduction by Adolfo Gilly (New York: Grove Press, 1967).

19.   Fanon's "Racism and Culture" appears in Frantz Fanon, *Toward the African Revolution: Political Essay*, ed. Jose Fanon, trans. Haakon Chevalier (New York: Grove Press, 1967).

20.   Paget Henry, *Caliban's Reason: Introducing Afro-Caribbean Philosophy* (New York: Routledge, 2000).

21.   Frantz Fanon, *The Wretched of the Earth*, trans. Constance Farrington (New York: Grove Press, 1962), 247.

22.   Ibid.

23.   In Ralph Ellison, *Shadow and Act* (New York: Vintage, 1964), 78–79.

24.   Alain Locke, "Values and Imperatives," 34.

8

On Palatable, Palliative, and Paralytic Affirmative Action, *Grutter*-Style

Ronald Turner

In its June 2003 decision in *Grutter v. Bollinger*, the United States Supreme Court addressed the question whether the University of Michigan Law School lawfully considered the race and ethnicity of applicants for admission to that institution as one factor in making admissions decisions. More specifically, the court asked whether the law school's pursuit of racial diversity in its student body was a compelling governmental interest justifying the use of race in selecting applicants for admission to that public university. Answering these questions in the affirmative, the court, by a 5-4 vote, held that the law school's narrowly tailored use of race did not violate the Equal Protection Clause of the Fourteenth Amendment to the United States Constitution or other federal antidiscrimination statutes.

This article discusses the Grutter Court's analysis of the important constitutional issue of race-conscious affirmative-action admissions in the higher education context, and the reasoning supporting the court's determination that the particular system promulgated and implemented by the law school passed constitutional muster. While the importance of the court's decision should not be doubted, this "stunning victory for affirmative action" (Stohr, 2004: 305) should not be overstated. I thus disagree with one writer's claim that *Grutter* is "the most important legal fight on racial discrimination in at least a generation" (Stohr, 2004: 5). Questioning that description and view, I argue herein that the court issued a palatable, palliative, and paralytic ruling. *Grutter* is palatable in the sense that the race-conscious activity before the court was "acceptable to the taste" and mind (Webster's, 2002: 1036) of pro-affirmative-action elites. *Grutter* is palliative and excusing and "lessen[s] the pain or severity ...

without actually curing" (*Webster's*, 2002:1037) the disease of racism. And *Grutter* is paralytic in that the court departed from, but left in place, the action-restrictive jurisprudence of its prior decisions which greatly limited, and in certain respects incapacitated, governmental entities as they responded to and moved against the moral enormity and legacies of slavery, Jim Crow, and the present-day manifestations of white supremacy (Brooks, 2004).

The Jurisprudential Backdrop

For a full understanding of why the particular form of affirmative action validated by the Supreme Court in *Grutter* is palatable, palliative, and paralytic, the discussion must begin with the court's seminal 1978 decision in *Regents of the University of California v. Bakke*. In that case the court considered Allan Bakke's challenge to the University of California at Davis medical school's "special admissions program." Bakke, a white male, had unsuccessfully applied for admission to the school (and had also been denied admission to twelve other medical schools (Jeffries, 1994; Selmi, 1999)). The at-issue admissions program reserved sixteen of one hundred seats in an entering class for applicants from economically and/or educationally disadvantaged individuals and for members of certain minority groups. Bakke alleged that the program excluded him because of his race and sought judicial relief, including a court order mandating his admission.

The court struck down the medical school's program and ordered Bakke's admission. Four justices (Justices Byron White, William Brennan, Thurgood Marshall, and Harry Blackmun) concluded that the Davis program was constitutional and did not violate the Equal Protection Clause. Four other justices (in an opinion by Justice John Paul Stevens joined by Chief Justice Warren Burger and Justices Potter Stewart and William Rehnquist) determined that Bakke should be admitted because the program took into account and discriminated on the basis of race in violation of Title VI of the Civil Rights Act of 1964. Justice Lewis Powell, speaking only for himself in a separate opinion, concluded (1) that the program's "line drawn on the basis of race and ethnic status" (*Bakke*: 289) violated both the Equal Protection Clause and Title VI, and (2) that race could be considered as a "plus" factor in the admissions process. Thus, five justices agreed that the program was illegal and ordered Bakke's admission, and five justices agreed that colleges and universities could lawfully consider race in admissions decisions. "What emerged as the 'rule' of the case was that universities may use race 'as a factor' in admissions but may not create quotas. But this rule represented the view of Justice Lewis Powell alone. The other eight justices explicitly rejected it. Ironically, the case stands for a proposition that only one justice thought sensible" (Sunstein, 2005: 144).

Justice Powell's views are of significance. As we will see, the court would endorse Powell's opinion twenty-five years later in *Grutter*. In Powell's view, the medical school's program classified persons on the basis of race and ethnicity and, in reserving sixteen of one hundred class seats for minority applicants (with minority applicants still competing for all one hundred seats), unlawfully limited white applicants to eighty-four class openings. Opining that "[r]acial and ethnic distinction of any sort are inherently suspect and thus call for the most exacting judicial examination," Powell had no difficulty in rejecting the school's argument that its "benign" affirmative-action measure was not premised on a suspect classification warranting heightened judicial scrutiny (*Bakke*: 291). "It is far too late to argue that the guarantee of equal protection to all persons permits the recognition of special wards entitled to a degree of protection greater than that accorded others" (295).

Erasing what he called the "artificial line of a 'two-class theory' of the Fourteenth Amendment," one dividing the world into a black minority and a white majority "itself . . . composed of various minority groups" (295), Justice Powell expressed his concern that preferential classifications of groups would require judicial evaluation and ranking of those groups on the basis of prejudices the groups experienced and the consequent harms suffered. In his view, the "kind of variable sociological and political analysis necessary to produce such rankings simply does not lie within the judicial competence—even if they otherwise were politically feasible and socially desirable" (297). Arguing, further, that there are "serious problems of justice connected with the idea of preference itself," Powell wrote that "preferential programs may only reinforce common stereotypes holding that certain groups are unable to achieve success without special protection based on a factor having no relationship to individual worth" (298). His perceived problematics of justice included what Powell described as "a measure of inequity in forcing innocent persons to bear the burdens of redressing grievances not of their making" (298). In the absence of a showing or findings of a constitutional or statutory violation justifying remedial action, government has no legitimate interest in helping minorities and "inflicting . . .

harm" on nonminorities "who bear no responsibility for whatever harm the beneficiaries of the special admissions program are thought to have suffered" (310). (Unlike Powell, Justices Brennan, White, Marshall, and Blackmun did not require a finding that a governmental entity had engaged in invidious racial discrimination (366 n.42).)

What, in Justice Powell's estimation, would be an acceptable form and goal of affirmative action? In a part of his opinion joined by no other justice, Powell identified student body diversity as a constitutionally permissible end for colleges and universities. Academic freedom "long has been viewed as a special concern of the First Amendment," he wrote, and the "freedom of a university to make its own judgments as to education includes the selection of its student body" (312). A diverse student body would promote an atmosphere of "speculation, experiment and creation" inside the university and would expose the nation's future leaders "to the ideas and mores of students as diverse as this Nation of many peoples" (312, 313). The medical school's goal of admitting and assembling "those students who will contribute the most to the 'robust exchange of ideas . . . is of paramount importance in the fulfillment of' the institution's mission," and would bring to the school qualified medical students from various backgrounds who "may bring to a professional school of medicine experiences, outlooks, and ideas that enrich the training of its student body and better equip its graduates to render with understanding their vital service to humanity" (314). Race could be considered in the pursuit of such diversity, Powell concluded, for "the State has a substantial interest that legitimately may be served by a properly devised admissions program involving the competitive consideration of race and ethnic origin" (320).

Compare and contrast Justice Powell's analysis with that set forth in Justice Marshall's separate opinion in *Bakke*. Detailing the historical mistreatment of African-Americans from slavery to modern times, Marshall argued that the "position of the Negro today in America is the tragic but inevitable consequence of centuries of unequal treatment. Measured by any benchmark of comfort or achievement, meaningful equality remains a distant dream for the Negro" (395). Contrary to Powell's universal Equal Protection Clause evenly applicable to all persons, Marshall understood that the intent and purpose of the Fourteenth Amendment was the protection of blacks from state discrimination; thus, for him, "it is inconceivable that the [amendment] was intended to prohibit all race-conscious relief measures" (398).

While Justice Marshall applauded the court's judgment, he complained that the court "ignores the fact that for several hundred years Negroes have been discriminated against, not as individuals, but rather solely because of the color of their skins" (410). Declaring that pervasive racism in the United States had touched all African-Americans "regardless of wealth or position" (400), the justice wrote:

> The experience of Negroes in America has been different in kind, not just in degree, from that of other ethnic groups. It is not merely the history of slavery alone but also that a whole people were marked as inferior by the law. And that mark has endured. The dream of America as the great melting pot has not been realized for the Negro; because of the color of his skin he never made it into the pot. (400-01)

Given that history and subordinating experience, Marshall found it "difficult . . . to accept that Negroes cannot be afforded greater protection under the Fourteenth Amendment where it is necessary to remedy the effects of past discrimination" (401).

> It is because of a legacy of unequal treatment that we must now permit the institutions of this society to give consideration to race in making decisions about who will hold the positions of influence, affluence, and prestige in America. For far too long, the doors to those positions have been shut to Negroes. If we are ever to become a fully integrated society, one in which the color of a person's skin will not determine the opportunities available to him or her, we must be willing to take steps to open those doors. I do not believe that anyone can truly look into America's past and still find that a remedy for the effects of that past is impermissible. (401-02)

Justice Powell and Justice Marshall thus differed in their views on and of the Equal Protection Clause as construed and applied to race-conscious affirmative action. For Powell, a one-size-fits-all clause provided constitutional protection for all of the nation's "minorities" (including groups and subgroups comprising the white majority), with no reference to or preference for African-Americans. While remedial programs and measures responsive to findings of constitutional and statutory violations were permissible, courts had to remain cognizant of the need to protect the "innocent" whose interests were adversely affected by affirmative action initiatives. Powell's remedial affirmative action is not a robust and minority-priority conception of affirmative action—African-Americans were viewed as just one of many groups, and "favoring" blacks cannot be done in ways that overlook or harm the interest of "innocent" whites (as compared to "guilty" beneficiaries? As Richard Delgado has asked, "Have you ever wondered what that makes us—if not innocent, then . . .?" (Delgado, 1991:124)). This rhetoric of white innocence sends the message that affirmative action measures "hurt innocent white people, and they advantage undeserving black people" (Ross, 1990: 301). Additionally, Powell endorsed instrumental affirmative action in which the consideration of race in furtherance of an institution's goals and mission for non-remedial purposes (such as the pursuit of student body racial and ethnic diversity and the perceived benefits thereof) is allowable.

Justice Marshall's affirmative action analysis rested on a different foundation reflecting his views of the particular circumstances of African-Americans subjected, as a group, to historical and contemporary race-based subordination. On that view, African-Americans are not just one of the nation's many minority groups protected by the Equal Protection Clause. While the equal protection mandate does apply to all persons, Marshall emphasized the protection-of-blacks provenance of a Fourteenth Amendment adopted to address and counteract the racist norm of posited black inferiority. From this perspective, and viewed through this prism, all "minorities" are not similarly situated for purposes of Equal Protection Clause analysis, as those on the black side of the black-white and black-nonblack divide were subjected to, and struggled and continue to struggle with and against, a virulent form of anti-black discrimination. Thus, as one commentator has noted, Marshall understood "that centuries of slavery and generations of legalized discrimination had left their mark on every black person on account of his race and so every black individual was both black and an individual" (Fried, 2004: 229). Affirmative action and reaction responsive to race-based and equality- and opportunity-limiting discrimination should and must be broadly reparative and not just narrowly remedial and instrumental. And the "innocents" whose interests must be protected and promoted are, not the whites focused on in Justice Powell's opinion, but those innocent persons of color who have been subjected to and/or marginalized by racism and white supremacy.

Free to select from a menu of remedial, instrumental, and reparative affirmative action, in subsequent cases the court chose the remedial model. For example, in *Wygant v. Jackson Board of Education* a plurality of the court ruled that a school board's policy protecting certain employees of color from layoffs because of their race or national origin violated the Equal Protection Clause. Justice Powell's opinion for the plurality rejected as insufficient the board's interest in providing minority role models for minority students and its efforts to address and alleviate the effects of societal (and not the school board's) discrimination. The role model theory, tying the desired percentage of minority teachers to the percentage of minority students, bore no relationship to any harm caused by discriminatory hiring practices, Powell reasoned, and could even be used to evade an obligation to remedy such practices where small percentages of black students were used to justify small percentages of black teachers. As for the societal discrimination rationale, Powell wrote that the "Court has never held that societal discrimination alone is sufficient to justify a racial classification" (*Wygant*: 274). "[T]he Court has insisted upon some showing of prior discrimination by the governmental unit involved before allowing limited use of racial classifications in order to remedy such discrimination" (274). "Societal discrimination, without more, is too amorphous a basis for imposing a racially classified remedy," and a court addressing such discrimination "could uphold remedies that are ageless in their reach into the past, and timeless in their ability to affect the future" (276).

The *Wygant* plurality further concluded that the school board's layoff policy had to be subjected to strict scrutiny review—the policy had to pursue a compelling governmental purpose accomplished by narrowly tailored means. Concerned (as he was in *Bakke*) about nonminorities burdened by affirmative action, Justice Powell argued that retaining minority teachers while laying off nonminority teachers with greater seniority placed "the entire burden of achieving racial equality on particular individuals, often resulting in serious disruption of their lives. That burden is too intrusive" (283). Unlike a valid hiring goal's diffusion of "the burden to be borne by innocent individuals," layoffs result in the "loss of an existing job" and "disrupt . . . settled expectations in a way that general hiring goals do not" (283). Thus, Powell concluded, while the purpose of promoting racial diversity in the teacher ranks may have been legitimate, the board's layoff-protection policy was not narrowly tailored to the accomplishment of that purpose and therefore violated the Equal Protection Clause.

In its 1989 decision in *City of Richmond v. Croson* the court struck down Richmond, Virginia's program requiring construction companies to subcontract a minimum of thirty percent of their contracts with the city with minority business enterprises (MBEs). The court, in an opinion by Justice Sandra Day O'Connor, subjected the program to strict scrutiny review and asked whether the MBE requirement was justified by a compelling governmental interest effectuated by narrowly tailored means. Strict scrutiny is employed to "'smoke out' illegitimate uses of race by assuring that [government] is pursuing a goal important enough to warrant use of a highly suspect tool" (493). This level of scrutiny of Richmond's program was necessary, in O'Connor's view, because:

blacks constitute approximately 50% of the population of the city of Richmond. Five of the nine seats on the city council are held by blacks. The concern that a political majority will more easily act to the disadvantage of a minority based on unwarranted assumptions or incomplete facts would seem to militate for, not against, the application of heightened judicial scrutiny in this case. (*Croson*: 495-96)

"This remarkable too-many-blacks observation" (Turner, 2003: 462) was criticized by Justice Marshall in his dissenting opinion:

The majority's view that remedial measures undertaken by municipalities with black leadership must face a stiffer test of Equal Protection Clause scrutiny than remedial measures undertaken by municipalities with white leadership implies a lack of political maturity on the part of this Nation's elected minority officials that is totally unwarranted. Such insulting judgments have no place in constitutional jurisprudence. (*Croson*: 555)

Richmond's set-aside program did not survive the court's scrutiny. With respect to the compelling governmental interest prong of the analysis, Justice O'Connor acknowledged "that the sorry history of both private and public discrimination in this country has contributed to a lack of opportunities for black entrepreneurs" (499). However, she concluded, past societal discrimination, standing alone and not "tied to any injury suffered by anyone," did not justify the MBE program's "rigid racial quota" (499). Indeed, she continued, recognition of past societal discrimination as a basis for racial preferences would "open the door to competing claims for 'remedial relief' for every disadvantaged group. The dream of a Nation of equal citizens in a society where race is irrelevant to personal opportunity and achievement would be lost in a mosaic of shifting preferences based on inherently unmeasurable claims of past wrongs" (505-06).

The program also failed to satisfy the court's narrow tailoring requirement as it was not apparent to Justice O'Connor that the city had considered race-neutral ways (such as city financing for small firms) to increase minority participation in contracting. O'Connor opined that the 30 percent set-aside "cannot be said to be narrowly tailored to any goal, except perhaps outright racial balancing. It rests upon the completely unrealistic assumption that minorities will choose a particular trade in lockstep proportion to their representation in the local population" (507). For these reasons, the court concluded that the program violated the Equal Protection Clause.

Croson's strict scrutiny of Richmond's affirmative action program was extended to a similar federal government initiative in *Adarand Constructors, Inc. v. Pena*. At issue in that case was the constitutionality of a United

States Department of Transportation program calling for the expenditure of 10 percent of department appropriations with small businesses owned and controlled by socially and economically disadvantaged individuals (who were presumptively African-American, Hispanic, Native American, Asian-Pacific-American, or a member of other minority groups).

Again writing for the court, Justice O'Connor referred to three propositions "lead[ing] to the conclusion that any person, of whatever race, has the right to demand that any governmental actor subject to the Constitution justify any racial classification subjecting that person to unequal treatment under the strictest judicial scrutiny" (Adarand: 224). First, preferences based on race or ethnicity should be viewed skeptically and "must necessarily receive a most searching examination." This examination is not "strict in theory, but fatal in fact," O'Connor cautioned, and determining whether a racial classification violates the Constitution "is the job of the court applying strict scrutiny" (237, 239-40). Second, the standard of judicial review in Equal Protection Clause cases must be consistent and "is not dependent on the race of those burdened or benefited by a particular classification . . ." (224). Third, congruency requires that judicial review of the federal government's actions under the Fifth Amendment to the Constitution be "the same as that under the Fourteenth Amendment" (224). "Taken together," O'Connor stated, "these three propositions lead to the conclusion that any person, of whatever race, has the right to demand that any governmental actor subject to the Constitution justify any racial classification subjecting that person to unequal treatment under the strictest judicial scrutiny" (224). Consequently, racial classifications "are constitutional only if they are narrowly tailored measures that further compelling governmental interests" (227).

Wygant, Croson, and *Adarand*—one employment case and two government contracting cases—dealt with, analyzed, and established the standard of judicial review of remedial affirmative action measures. Given the court's focus on the question whether the governmental bodies in those cases pursued a compelling interest in remedying discrimination through narrowly tailored means, the legality of the non-remedial diversity justification for race-conscious affirmative action became a point of contention. For instance, in *Hopwood v. Texas* the United States Court of Appeals for the Fifth Circuit held that consideration of race or ethnicity for the purpose of achieving student body diversity was not a compelling interest under the Fourteenth Amendment. In so holding, the court reasoned that it was not bound by the Supreme Court's decision in *Bakke:*

[T]here has been no indication from the Supreme Court, other than Justice Powell's lonely opinion in *Bakke*, that the state's interest in diversity constitutes a compelling justification for governmental race-based discrimination. Subsequent Supreme Court caselaw strongly suggests, in fact, that it is not. (*Hopwood*: 945)

Disagreeing with that view, one of the Fifth Circuit's judges argued that "if *Bakke* is to be declared dead, the Supreme Court, not a three-judge panel of a circuit court, should make that pronouncement" (963). And a 2000 decision by the United States Court of Appeals for the Ninth Circuit, in *Smith v. University of Washington Law School*, validated the consideration of race in admissions decisions and urged that a majority of the Bakke Court "would have allowed for some race-based considerations in educational institutions. Thus, a race-based possibility must be taken to be the actual rationale adopted by the Court" (Smith: 1199). This conflict between the Ninth Circuit and the Fifth Circuit was resolved by the Supreme Court in 2003.

Grutter

In 1996 Barbara Grutter submitted an application for admission to the University of Michigan Law School. When her application was denied, Grutter, a white resident of the state of Michigan, sued the law school and alleged that she had been discriminated against on the basis of race in violation of the Fourteenth Amendment and other federal antidiscrimination laws. Grutter challenged the law school's official and declared policy of considering "racial and ethnic diversity with special reference to the inclusion of students from groups which have been historically discriminated against, like African-Americans, Hispanics and Native Americans, who without this commitment might not be represented in our student body in meaningful numbers" (*Grutter*: 316). According to Grutter, her application was rejected because race was a predominant factor in the law school's admissions process and certain minority applicants had "a significantly greater chance of admission than students with similar credentials from disfavored racial groups" (317).

Grutter's arguments did not persuade a majority of the nine Supreme Court justices. Speaking for herself and Justices John Paul Stevens, David Souter, Ruth Bader Ginsburg, and Stephen Breyer, Justice O'Connor "endorse[d] Justice Powell's view [in *Bakke*] that student body diversity is a compelling state interest that can justify the use of race in university admissions" (325). While such use of race is subject to the most rigorous level of judicial review, O'Connor, quoting from her *Adarand* opinion, stated that strict scrutiny is "not 'strict in theory, but fatal in fact'" and that not all governmental consideration of race is invalid (327).

According to Justice O'Connor, "Context matters when reviewing race-based governmental action under the Equal Protection Clause" (327). Having posited a contextual equal protection analysis, she made clear that the court's post-*Bakke* decisions (see *Wygant*, *Croson*, and *Adarand*) did not limit affirmative action to government efforts to remedy past discrimination. (In rejecting this restriction O'Connor conceded, correctly, that language in the court's prior decisions "might be read to suggest that remedying past discrimination is the only permissible justification for race-based governmental action" (328).) "Today, we hold that the Law School has a compelling interest in attaining a diverse student body" (328). Deferring to the institution's educational judgment, and presuming that the school acted in good faith, O'Connor opined that the "critical mass" of minority students the school sought to admit and enroll was defined by substantial educational benefits, including the promotion of "cross-racial understanding" and breaking down racial stereotypes (330). The court thus accepted instrumental and operational affirmative action and the proposition that racial and ethnic diversity were important to and furthered the law school's goals, aspirations, and internal functions.

Of especial relevance to this article's thesis is the court's recognition of interests "beyond the walls and halls" of the university (Turner, 2004:211). Justice O'Connor cited *amicus curiae* briefs submitted to the court by major American corporations extolling the benefits of diversity. (More on these briefs below.) "These benefits are not theoretical but real, as major American businesses have made clear that the skills needed in today's increasingly global marketplace can only be developed through exposure to widely diverse people, cultures, ideas, and viewpoints" (*Grutter*: 330). Moreover, and going beyond this entrepreneurial rationale for affirmative action, O'Connor pointed to another friend-of-the-court brief filed by former high-ranking officers in, and civilian leaders of, the nation's military in which the national security benefits of diversity were identified. This brief argued (and O'Connor agreed) that a racially diverse officer corps, drawn primarily from the service academies and the Reserve Officer Training Corps, "is essential to the nation's ability to fulfill its princip[al] mission to provide national security" (331).

Acknowledging "the overriding importance of preparing students for work and citizenship" and quoting *Brown v. Board of Education's* declaration that "education . . . is the very foundation of good citizenship"

(*Brown*: 493), Justice O'Connor emphasized that "public institutions of higher education must be accessible to all individuals regardless of race or ethnicity. . . . Effective participation by members of all racial and ethnic groups in the civic life of our Nation is essential if the dream of one Nation, indivisible, is to be realized" (*Grutter*: 331-32). Why, in the court's view, was this access and participation important?

> In order to cultivate a set of leaders with legitimacy in the eyes of the citizenry, it is necessary that the path to leadership be visibly open to talented and qualified individuals of every race and ethnicity. All members of our heterogeneous society must have confidence in the openness and integrity of the educational institutions that provide this training. . . . Access to legal education (and thus the legal profession) must be inclusive of talented and qualified individuals of every race and ethnicity, so that all members of our heterogeneous society may participate in the educational institutions that provide the training and education necessary to succeed in America. (332-33)

Having found that the law school had a compelling interest in student body diversity, the court turned to the question of whether that interest was effectuated through narrowly tailored means. Answering that question in the affirmative, Justice O'Connor noted that the challenged admissions policy considered race or ethnicity as a plus factor along with a number of other non-racial factors assessed in a "holistic" review of each applicant's file. (The law school did not automatically and mechanically award a set number of points for minority status as the University of Michigan did in its undergraduate admissions decisions; that policy was struck down by the court in *Gratz v. Bollinger*.) In fact, nonminority applicants were often admitted over minority applicants with higher grades and Law School Admissions Test (LSAT) scores. In addition, and in accordance with the court's analysis in *Croson*, O'Connor considered the argument that the school unlawfully failed to exhaust all race-neutral alternatives (such as a lottery admissions system or less emphasis on grades and LSAT scores) before adopting its race-conscious policy. She pointed out that such exhaustion is not required by narrow tailoring, and that a university is not required "to choose between maintaining a reputation for excellence or fulfilling a commitment to provide educational opportunities to members of all groups" (339).

In the final pages of her opinion Justice O'Connor turned to the issue of time limitations for race-conscious affirmative action programs. Believing "that all governmental use of race must have a logical end point," she wrote that "the durational requirement can be met by sunset provisions in race-conscious admissions policies and periodic reviews to determine whether racial preferences are still necessary to achieve student body diversity" (342).

> It has been 25 years since Justice Powell first approved the use of race to further an interest in student body diversity in the context of public higher education. Since that time, the number of minority applicants with high grades and test scores has indeed increased. . . . We expect that 25 years from now, the use of racial preferences will no longer be necessary to further the interests approved today. (343)

In sum, the court saw no constitutional flaw in Michigan's determination that racial and ethnic diversity in its student body benefited the law school, could promote understanding between students of different races, could address the operational needs of the nation's major businesses competing in a global economy, and could facilitate the diversification of the military's officer corps. Moreover, the court opined that the diversity-based affirmative action of the kind pursued by the elite Michigan law school legitimates the nation's leadership in the sense that legal education and the legal profession are not racially and ethnically segregated and are open to a heterogeneous body of qualified and talented persons. As these concerns were not invalid as a matter of constitutional law, Barbara Grutter's challenge to the law school's affirmative action policy failed.

Palatable, Palliative, and Paralytic Affirmative Action

An evaluation of *Grutter* must and should begin with an assessment of the various conceptions and meanings of race-conscious affirmative action, for only then can the significance and impact of the court's decision be accurately and meaningfully critiqued. As noted in the previous sections of this article, affirmative action can be categorized as remedial, reparative, instrumental, operational, and entrepreneurial. The constitutionality of the remedial model, coupled with strict judicial review of governmental consideration and use of race or ethnicity, has been firmly established in the court's jurisprudence. The reparative model, favored and promoted by Justice Marshall in his *Bakke* opinion, did not gain a foothold in the court's jurisprudence. And in *Grutter* the court recognized (indeed, embraced) the instrumental, operational, and entrepreneurial models of affirmative action in the specific context of an elite law school's consideration of race in its admissions process and decisions.

Consider two meanings of affirmative action offered by Charles Lawrence and Mari Matsuda: shallow meaning and deep meaning:

> The shallow meaning goes something like this: there were once laws and practices that denied people of color access to schools, jobs, and housing. There was a need to make sure that these explicit practices of segregation and discrimination ended. The practices were mistakes and things done by a few bad people. We regret them and will invite a few token persons from minority communities into our institutions

to make up for that mistake. We also recognize that it would help the children of the powerful to learn more about the nonwhite world if a few nonwhites were around, but we will decide whom to invite. We will decide who is qualified to serve our purpose of creating an environment where we can learn what we need to know about them. (Lawrence and Matsuda, 1997:27)

Deep meaning affirmative action, by contrast:

is radically different and recognizes that the only remedy for racial subordination based on the systemic disestablishment of structures, institutions, and ideologies is the systemic disestablishment of those structures, institutions, and ideologies. Radical affirmative action goes beyond the remedy of simply declaring that discrimination is illegal and pretending that our culture is colorblind. It says that it is not enough for the discriminator to remove his foot from the victim's throat and call it equal opportunity. (27)

Thus, Lawrence and Matsuda argue, the "shallow version of affirmative action is an attempt by those with privilege to buy their way out cheap, to create an illusion of justice overlaying growing divisions between have and have not" (29). That version of affirmative action "serves as a homeostatic device, assuring that only a small number of women and people of color are hired or promoted. Not too many, for that would be terrifying, nor too few, for that would be destabilizing. Just the right small number, generally those who need it least, are moved ahead" (Delgado, 1991: 1224). On that view, affirmative action "play[s] a negative role—namely, to ensure that discriminatory practices against women and people of color are abated" (West, 1993, 2001: 64). The deep version, by contrast, does not seek "to educate white folks and serve elite white interests" and "recognize[s] that racist institutions remain racist as long as they serve the exploiters of oppressed communities. It recognizes that those who are privileged by race and gender cannot judge who is best qualified to engage in the struggle against that privilege" (Lawrence and Matsuda, 1997: 28).

Grutter is not and can in no way be described as radical or deep meaning affirmative action. In fact, as Bryan Fair has remarked, *Grutter* "is conservative. It portends little change in educational access" (Fair, 2004:1851). In maintaining the status quo the court "does not mandate that more minority students must be enrolled at the nation's flagship schools" and does not "declare that the disproportionate educational advantages that whites receive at the top public schools are unconstitutional" (Fair, 2005: 761). This conservatism does not mean that supporters of diversity-based affirmative action did not win an important battle. But that isolated victory must not be confused or conflated with the ongoing struggle and battle in the larger war against conditions caused by and related to the ravages of racism and white supremacy: black incarceration rates, poverty, unemployment, substandard educational opportunities, segregated housing patterns and the like (Edwards, 2004: 967-68; Loury, 2002: 122-23). Affirmative action *Grutter*-style does not address these entrenched problems and issues facing far too many in African-American communities.

Grutter is, therefore, palatable. In accepting instrumental, operational, and entrepreneurial affirmative action the court explained that affirmative action is beneficial for the nation's elite colleges and universities and is good for big business. For those concerned about or opposed to race-conscious affirmative action, the court's utilitarian analysis is (relatively) tastier and easier to swallow than an approach founded on a frank (and for many jarring and uncomfortable) account chronicling racism past and present. And any doubt that the court's principal focus was on elite (and not all) universities is dispelled by its description of the University of Michigan Law School as "among the Nation's top law schools" (*Grutter*: 312), and by Justice O'Connor's selection and reliance on the amicus briefs submitted to the court by large American corporations. Those briefs urged that individuals educated in the country's "leading institutions of higher education" promote the internal workforce and external marketing interests of business (Brief for 65 Leading American Businesses, 2003: 7), and that "[s]elective universities and colleges serve as training grounds for and gateways to the higher echelons of all realms of American society, including corporate America" (Brief of General Motors, 2003: 22). Notably, these "briefs were forward-looking and ... utilitarian. They were silent on the subject of discrimination" (Brown-Nagin, 2005: 1464). Indeed, as reported by Mark Tushnet, Justice John Paul Stevens told his colleagues on the court that they "should rely on 'the accumulated wisdom of the country's leaders,' as reflected in the amicus briefs" (Tushnet, 2005: 234).

That the court agreed with and validated the views of the law school and major businesses is not surprising given the court's history of reflecting the preferences of certain elites (Spann, 1993:19; Balkin, 2003:1538; Devins, 2003:351). Moreover, *Grutter* is an instructive exemplar of Derrick Bell's interest-convergence theory (Bell, 1980; Green, 2005:959). This theory posits that the "interest of blacks in achieving racial equality will be accommodated only when it converges with the interests of whites" (Bell, 1980: 523). Thus, Bell argues, "no matter how much harm blacks were suffering because of racial hostility and discrimination, we could not obtain meaningful relief until policymakers perceived that the relief blacks sought furthered interests or resolved issues of more primary concern" (West, 2003: 1624). Furthermore, the focus on diversity avoids the affirmative-action-hurts-innocent-whites concern expressed in the court's remedial affirmative action decisions. If diversity benefits whites admitted to elite institutions of higher education, the public goods of affirmative action are distributed among whites and not just between white and black racial groups; consequently, whites and not just blacks are the beneficiaries of affirmative action (Skrentny, 1996: 228). "Diversity discourse thus disavows the racial 'us against them' mentality of affirmative action discourse" (Flagg, 2004: 849).

Grutter is a palliative court ruling. The focus on and the energy devoted to the efforts of elite colleges and universities to promote diversity in their student bodies, while of obvious importance to a number of people of color desiring and seeking access to those institutions, alleviates some of the pain of (but does not cure) the disease of racism and white supremacy. The negative manifestations of that disease will continue to adversely affect the lives and life opportunities of far too many in Aframerica and will not be optimally or effectively addressed or redressed by incremental advances in university admissions policies. To the extent that diversity becomes the primary, if not the exclusive, focus of both sides of the affirmative action debate, the conversation is moved away from racial justice concerns and reparative initiatives and toward more conservative and, as previously discussed, more agreeable propositions, that is, instrumental, operational, and entrepreneurial diversity. While diversity as a pain reliever is important, institutional resort to and judicial endorsement of this tool is not curative—the opportunity-enervating disease of race and racism remain.

Grutter is paralytic—the court left in place its prior decisions holding that past societal discrimination does not justify race-conscious affirmative action measures. As Justice Stephen Breyer writes in his recently published book, the Michigan law school "did not press this kind of equality-based remedial claim strongly. Its hesitancy may have reflected the fact that the Court in earlier cases cast doubt on the constitutional validity of affirmative action that seeks to remedy 'prior societal discrimination'" (Breyer, 2005: 80). Expressing the same view, Derrick Bell contends that "Michigan lawyers and their civil rights allies shifted the focus from remediation for past discrimination to the value of diversity to the schools and to society" (Bell, 2003: 1624-25). It is also noteworthy that the Grutter Court accepted and did not question the conception of "merit" as measured by LSAT scores and grade point averages. (Interestingly, in his *Grutter* dissent Justice Clarence Thomas, an opponent of affirmative action, argued that "there is much to be said for the view that the use of tests and other measures to 'predict' academic performance is a poor substitute for a system that gives every applicant a chance to prove he can succeed in the study of law" (*Grutter*: 367)). If, as I believe, "there is a limit to what numbers can forecast about the things we value in people and education" (Edwards, 2004:969), one should not expect transformative or even significant increases in minority admissions where diversity initiatives operate within a still entrenched regime of numbers-based meritocracy in elite colleges and universities.

Conclusion

Grutter is an important victory for proponents of race-conscious affirmative action in college and university admissions. The court made clear that the consideration of race as a (and not the only) factor in a holistic and individualized review of an applicant's file does not violate the Equal Protection Clause. As argued in the preceding pages, the court's palatable, palliative, and paralytic decision is a limited one addressing and validating diversity-based affirmative action in the specific context of admissions in the elite professional school setting. Affirmative action, *Grutter*-style, is instrumental, operational, and entrepreneurial. Affirmative action, *Grutter*-style, is not reparative and, when viewed in the context of and measured against "the brutal harms inflicted by slavery and Jim Crow" (Katznelson, 2005:157), is conservative and cautious. Affirmative action, *Grutter*-style, is not about corrective justice pursued by those who seek to "put an end to the caste status of blacks in American life, and thus also to put an end to white privilege, or another such lofty goal . . ." (Katznelson, 2005: 158). Affirmative action, *Grutter*-style, is palatable, palliative, and paralytic.

References

Adarand Constructors, Inc. v. Pena, 515 U.S. 200 (1995).

Balkin, J.M. (2003). "What *Brown* Teaches Us About Constitutional Theory." *Virginia Law Review*, 90:1537-77.

Bell, D. (2003). "Diversity's Distractions." *Columbia Law Review*, 103:1622-33.

Bell, D. (1980). "*Brown v. Board of Education* and the Interest-Convergence Dilemma." *Harvard Law Review*, 93:518-33.

Breyer, S. (2005). *Active Liberty: Interpreting Our Democratic Constitution*. New York: Alfred A. Knopf.

Brief for 65 Leading American Businesses in Support of Respondents (Feb. 2003), United States Supreme Court.

Brief of General Motors Corporation as Amicus Curiae in Support of Respondents (Feb. 2003), United States Supreme Court.

Brooks, R. (2004). *Atonement and Forgiveness: A New Model for Black Reparations*. Berkeley: University of California Press.

Brown v. Board of Education, 347 U.S. 483 (1954).

Brown-Nagin, T. (2005). "Elites, Social Movements, and the Law: The Case for Affirmative Action." *Columbia Law Review*, 105:1436-1528.

City of Richmond v. Croson, 488 U.S. 469 (1989).

Delgado, R. (1991). "Affirmative Action as a Majoritarian Device: Or, Do You Really Want to be a Role Model?" *Michigan Law Review*, 89: 1222-1231.

Devins, N. (2003). "Explaining *Grutter v. Bollinger*." *University of Pennsylvania Law Review*, 152:347-83.

Edwards, H. (2004). "The Journey from *Brown v. Board of Education* to *Grutter v. Bollinger*: From Racial Assimilation to Diversity." *Michigan Law Review*, 102:944-78.

Fair, B. (2005). "Re(caste)ing Equality Theory: Will *Grutter* Survive Itself by 2028?" *University of Pennsylvania Journal of Constitutional Law*, 7:721-63.

Fair, B. (2004). "Taking Educational Caste Seriously: Why *Grutter* Will Help Very Little." *Tulane Law Review*, 78:1843-75.

Flagg, B. (2004). "Diversity Discourses." *Tulane Law Review*, 78:827-51.

Fried, C. (2004). *Saying What the Law Is: The Constitution in the Supreme Court*. Cambridge: Harvard University Press.

Gratz v. Bollinger, 539 U.S. 244 (2003).

Green, M. (2005). "Addressing Race Discrimination under Title VII after Forty Years: The Promise of ADR as Interest-Convergence." *Howard Law Journal*, 48:937-70.

Grutter v. Bollinger, 539 U.S. 306 (2003).

Hopwood v. Texas, 78 F.3d 932 (5th Cir. 1996).

Jeffries, J. (1994). *Justice Lewis F. Powell, Jr.: A Biography*. New York: Scribner.

Katznelson, I. (2005). *When Affirmative Action Was White*. New York: W.W. Norton.

Lawrence, C. and M.J. Matsuda. (1997). *We Won't Go Back: Making the Case for Affirmative Action*. New York: Houghton Mifflin.

Loury, G. (2002). *The Anatomy of Racial Inequality*. Cambridge: Harvard University Press.

Ross, T. (1990). "Innocence and Affirmative Action." *Vanderbilt Law Review*, 43:297-316.

Regents of the University of California v. Bakke, 438 U.S. 265 (1978).

Selmi, M. (1999). "The Life of *Bakke*: An Affirmative Action Retrospective." *Georgetown Law Journal*, 87: 981-1021.

Skrentny, J. (1996). *The Ironies of Affirmative Action: Politics, Culture, and Justice in America*. Chicago: University of Chicago Press.

Smith v. University of Washington Law School, 233 F.3d 1188 (9th Cir. 2000).

Spann, G. (1993). *Race Against the Court: The Supreme Court and Minorities in Contemporary America*. New York: New York University Press.

Stohr, G. (2004). *A Black and White Case: How Affirmative Action Survived Its Greatest Challenge*. Princeton, NJ: Bloomberg Press.

Sunstein, C. (2005). *Radicals in Robes: Why Extreme Right-Wing Courts Are Wrong for America*. New York: Basic Books.

Turner, R. (2004). "*Grutter*, the Diversity Justification, and Workplace Affirmative Action." *Brandeis Law Journal*, 43:200-37.

Turner, R. (2003). "The Too-Many Minorities and Racegoating Dynamics of the Anti-Affirmative-Action Position: From *Bakke* to *Grutter* and Beyond." *Hastings Constitutional Law Quarterly*, 30:445-510.

Tushnet, M. (2005). *A Court Divided: The Rehnquist Court and the Future of Constitutional Law*. New York: W.W. Norton.

Webster's New World College Dictionary. Fourth ed. 2002. Cleveland: Wiley Publishing, Inc.

West, C. (1993, 2001). *Race Matters*. Boston: Beacon Press.

Wygant v. Jackson Board of Education, 476 U.S. 267 (1986).

Contributors

Delores P. Aldridge, Ph.D., is the Grace Towns Hamilton Professor of Sociology and African American Studies at Emory University. Her research area of emphasis is on: Africana Theory; black male-female relationships; and cultural democracy. She is the coeditor of *Out of the Revelation: The Development for African Studies.*

Cecil A. Blake, Ph.D., is an Associate Professor of Black Studies and the chair to the Department of Black Studies at the University of Pittsburgh. He is the coeditor of the book titled, *Intercultural Communication: Roots & Routes*, 1998.

James L. Conyers, Jr., Ph.D., is a University Professor of African American Studies and Director of the African American Studies Program and Director of the Center of African American Culture at the University of Houston. His most recent publication is entitled, *Engines of the Black Power Movement* (2007), McFarland Publishers.

Lewis R. Gordon, Ph.D., is a Laura H. Carnell Professor of Philosophy and Director, Institute for the Study of Race and Social Thought at Temple University. He is the author of over 10 books. His recent forthcoming publication is titled, *An Introduction to Africana Philosophy*, Cambridge, U.K.: Cambridge University Press, 2007.

Winston Van Horne, Ph.D., is a Professor of Africology at the University of Wisconsin at Milwaukee. His research area of expertise is in political science. He is the author of several scholarly articles.

Ula Y. Taylor, Ph.D., is an Associate Professor of African American Studies at University of California at Berkeley. She is the author of numerous scholarly articles and the books titled, coauthor of *Panther: A Pictorial History of the Black Panthers and the Story Behind the Film (1995)*; *The Veiled Garvey (2002)*; and *Re-Gendering a Nation: A History of the Nation of Islam* (forthcoming).

Ronald Turner, J.D., is Alumnae Law Center Professor of Law at the University of Houston's Law Center. He is the author of several articles and the book titled, *Working While Black—African Americans, the Workplace, and the Law,* New York University Press, 2000.

Robert E. Weems Jr., Ph.D., is a Professor of History at University of Missouri at Columbia.   He is the author of: *Desegregating the Dollar* (1998); *Black Business in the Black Metropolis* (1996); and coeditor of *The African American Experience.*

Index